GRAMMAR

BEAN

4

지은이	NE능률 영어교육연구소
선임연구원	김지현
연구원	이지영 차연경
영문 교열	Nathaniel Galletta August Niederhaus
디자인	박정진 오솔길 김명진
내지 일러스트	정경호
내지 사진	www.shutterstock.com
맥편집	김선희

NE능률이
미래를
창조합니다.

건강한 배움의 고객가치를 제공하겠다는 꿈을 실현하기 위해
40년이 넘는 시간 동안 열심히 달려왔습니다.

앞으로도 끊임없는 연구와 노력을 통해
당연한 것을 멈추지 않고

고객, 기업, 직원 모두가 함께 성장하는 NE능률이 되겠습니다.

Beginning

Easy

Active

New

이제 시작이에요!
처음으로 문법을 공부하는 여러분, 두려워하지 마세요.
이제부터 Grammar Bean(그래머빈)이 영어에 대한
자신감을 가질 수 있게 도와줄게요.

구성과 특징

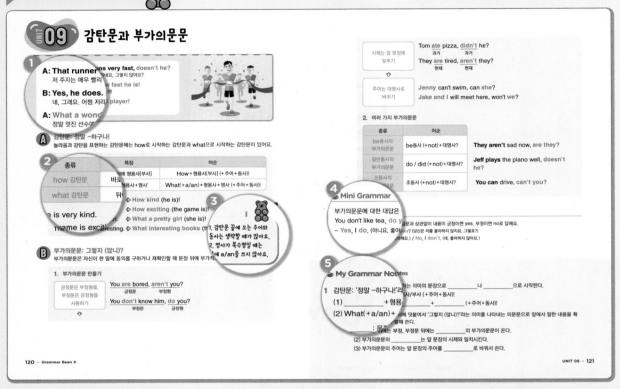

알기 쉬운 문법 설명

09 감탄문과 부가의문문

1

A: That runner ___ns very fast, doesn't he?
저 주자는 매우 빨리 ___네요. 그렇지 않아요?
___w fast he is!
B: Yes, he does. ___까
네, 그래요. 어쩜 저러 ___ player!
A: What a wond ___
정말 멋진 선수 ___

A 감탄문: 정말 ~하구나!
놀라움과 감탄을 표현하는 감탄문에는 how로 시작하는 감탄문과 what으로 시작하는 감탄문이 있어요.

2

종류	특징	어순
how 감탄문	___에 형용사[부사] 바로	How+형용사[부사] (+주어+동사)!
what 감탄문	형용사+명사 뒤에	What(+a/an)+형용사+명사 (+주어+동사)!

___e is very kind. ⇨ How kind (he is)!
___name is exciting. ⇨ How exciting (the game is)!
⇨ What a pretty girl (she is)!
⇨ What interesting books (th __

3
1. 감탄문 끝에 오는 주어와 동사는 생략할 때가 많아요.
2. 명사가 복수형일 때는 ___에 a/an을 쓰지 않아요.

B 부가의문문: 그렇지 (않니)?
부가의문문은 자신이 한 말에 동의를 구하거나 재확인할 때 문장 뒤에 부가적 ___

1. 부가의문문 만들기

| 긍정문은 부정형을, 부정문은 긍정형을 사용하기 | You are bored, aren't you? 긍정문 부정형 |
| | You don't know him, do you? 부정문 긍정형 |

시제는 앞 문장에 맞추기
Tom ate pizza, didn't he?
과거 과거
They are tired, aren't they?
현재 현재

주어는 대명사로 바꾸기
Jenny can't swim, can she?
Jake and I will meet here, won't we?

2. 여러 가지 부가의문문

종류	어순	
be동사의 부가의문문	be동사 (+not)+대명사?	They aren't sad now, are they?
일반동사의 부가의문문	do / did (+not)+대명사?	Jeff plays the piano well, doesn't he?
조동사의 ___	조동사 (+not)+대명사?	You can drive, can't you?

4 Mini Grammar
부가의문문에 대한 대답은
You don't like tea, do y ___ ___문과 상관없이 내용이 긍정이면 yes, 부정이면 no로 답해요.
– Yes, I do. (아니요, 좋아 ___?(당신은 차를 좋아하지 않지요, 그렇죠?)
___해요.) / No, I don't. (네, 좋아하지 않아요.)

5 My Grammar Notes
1 감탄문: '정말 ~하구나'라 ___는 의미의 문장으로 ___나 ___으로 시작한다.
(1) ___ +형용 ___사/부사 (+주어+동사)!
(2) What(+a/an)+ ___ + ___ (+주어+동사)!
___ 뒤에 덧붙여서 '그렇지 (않니)?'라는 의미를 나타내는 의문문으로 앞에서 말한 내용을 확 ___할 때 쓴다.
: 문장 ___
___ ___ 문에는 부정, 부정문 뒤에는 ___의 부가의문문이 온다.
(2) 부가의문문의 ___은 앞 문장의 시제와 일치시킨다.
(3) 부가의문문의 주어는 앞 문장의 주어를 ___로 바꿔서 쓴다.

1 간단한 예문을 살펴보면서 학습할 내용을 예상해 보세요.

2 한눈에 들어오는 문법 정리와 예문으로 문법 내용을 쉽게 이해할 수 있어요.

3 말풍선 안에는 주의해야 하거나 꼭 기억해야 할 내용이 있으니 꼼꼼히 챙겨 보세요.

4 Mini Grammar에서는 지금 공부하는 내용과 관련하여 추가적으로 알면 도움이 되는 문법 사항이 제시되어 있어요.

5 My Grammar Notes는 학습한 내용을 정리하는 코너예요. 빈칸을 채우면서 요점을 정리해 보세요.

다양한 유형의 3단계 Exercise + Test

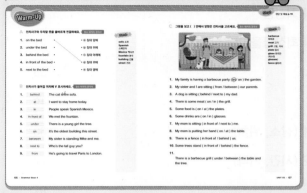

Warm-Up
새롭게 학습한 내용을 충분히 이해했나요? 간단한 문제를 통해 점검해 보세요.

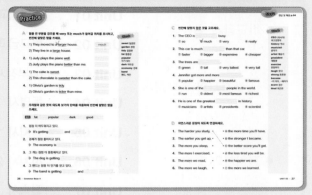

Practice
연습이 최선이라는 말 알고 있죠? 다양하고 많은 연습문제를 풀면서 자연스럽게 문법을 익힐 수 있어요.

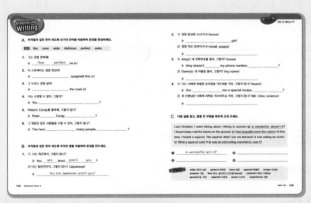

Grammar into Writing
문법을 배우는 목적이 문제 풀이와 시험만은 아니에요. 문법을 활용하면 영어 문장을 쓰는 것도 문제 없어요.

Wrap-Up Test
객관식 문제와 서술형 문제를 통해 배운 내용을 총정리해 보세요. 점수가 좋지 않으면 복습을 잊지 마세요.

+ Workbook

각 Unit별 연습문제와 별도의 Grammar Test가 수록되어 있어요.
Workbook을 통해 부족한 부분을 보충하고 배운 내용을 내 것으로 만들어 보세요.

CONTENTS

STUDY PLAN

차시	진도 현황 (교재)		숙제 (Workbook)	학습 날짜	복습 (O/X)	어휘 (전/후)
1차시	Unit 01	비교급과 최상급		월 일		개
2차시				월 일		개
3차시	Unit 02	비교급과 최상급을 이용한 표현		월 일		
4차시				월 일		
5차시	Unit 03	to부정사		월 일		
6차시				월 일		
7차시	Unit 04	동명사		월 일		
8차시				월 일		
9차시	Unit 05	전치사 1 (장소, 위치)		월 일		
10차시				월 일		
11차시	Unit 06	전치사 2 (시간, 기타)		월 일		
12차시				월 일		
13차시	Unit 07	접속사		월 일		
14차시				월 일		
15차시	Unit 08	명령문과 제안문		월 일		
16차시				월 일		
17차시	Unit 09	감탄문과 부가의문문		월 일		
18차시				월 일		
19차시	Unit 10	부정의문문과 선택의문문		월 일		
20차시				월 일		

① 숙제 칸에는 숙제 내용을 적고, 학습 날짜 칸에는 수업 날짜를 적어요.

② 오답 복습을 완료하면 복습 칸에 동그라미(O) 표시를 해요.

③ 학습하기 전 모르는 어휘 개수를 칸 왼쪽에 적고, 학습 후 틀린 어휘 개수를 칸 오른쪽에 적어요.
(www.nebooks.co.kr에서 어휘 리스트를 받아 공부하세요!)

UNIT 01

비교급

최상급

🥒 **Vocab Check!** 이번 과에서 배울 단어의 뜻을 확인하고, 모르는 단어에 체크 표시하세요.

✔ 1	diligent	형 부지런한		11	friendship	명 우정		21	weigh	통 무게가 ~이다
2	interesting	형 흥미로운		12	turtle	명 거북이		22	useful	형 유용한
3	soldier	명 군인		13	light	형 가벼운		23	careful	형 조심하는, 주의 깊은
4	expensive	형 (값이) 비싼		14	problem	명 문제		24	player	명 선수; 연주자
5	important	형 중요한		15	shirt	명 셔츠		25	active	형 활동적인, 적극적인
6	subject	명 과목		16	earth	명 지구		26	deep	형 깊은
7	moment	명 순간		17	next	형 다음의		27	ocean	명 바다, 해양
8	joke	명 농담		18	cozy	형 아늑한		28	warm	형 따뜻한
9	accident	명 사고		19	island	명 섬		29	kite	명 연
10	grade	명 점수, 성적		20	way	명 방법		30	lazy	형 게으른

UNIT 01 비교급과 최상급

Mr. Brown is old.
Brown 씨는 나이가 많아요.

He is older than my grandfather.
그는 나의 할아버지보다 나이가 많아요.

He is the oldest person in this town.
그는 이 마을에서 나이가 가장 많은 사람이에요.

 비교급, 최상급 만들기

1. 규칙적인 변화

	비교급/최상급	단어	비교급 (더 ~한/하게)	최상급 (가장 ~한/하게)
대부분의 단어	단어+**er** 단어+**est**	old (나이가 든) long (긴)	older longer	oldest longest
-e로 끝나는 단어	단어+**r** 단어+**st**	safe (안전한) nice (멋진)	safer nicer	safest nicest
-y로 끝나는 단어	y 없애고 **-ier** y 없애고 **-iest**	heavy (무거운) easy (쉬운)	heavier easier	heaviest easiest
모음1개, 자음1개로 끝나는 단어	단어+끝자음+**-er** 단어+끝자음+**-est**	big (큰) hot (뜨거운, 더운)	bigger hotter	biggest hottest
길이가 긴 단어	**more**+단어 **most**+단어	famous (유명한) popular (인기 있는)	**more** famous **more** popular	**most** famous **most** popular

2. 불규칙적인 변화 참고 4권 부록

good (좋은) / well (잘) – **better** – **best**   bad (나쁜) – **worse** – **worst**

little (작은, 적은) – **less** – **least**   many, much (많은) – **more** – **most**

B 비교급＋than: ~보다 더 …한[하게]

두 가지 대상을 비교할 때는 형용사[부사]의 비교급 형태와 than을 사용해서 나타내요.
than 뒤에 비교 대상을 써요.

taller ((키/높이가) 더 큰) **larger** ((크기가) 더 큰) **hotter** (더 더운, 더 뜨거운) **more carefully** (더 주의 깊게)	**+**	**than** (~보다)

'나보다'라고 할 때는 than I와 than me 둘 다 쓸 수 있어요.

Mike is **taller than** me.   Canada is **larger than** the U.S.
Summer is **hotter than** spring.   She drives **more carefully than** I.

C the＋최상급＋in/of ~: ~(중)에서 가장 …한[하게]

여러 대상 중에 으뜸가는 것을 나타낼 때는 최상급을 사용해요. 보통 in 뒤에는 장소·단체 이름이 오고,
of 뒤에는 사물(사람)이나 일정 기간을 나타내는 말이 이어져요.

the	**+**	**best** (최고의) **fastest** (가장 빠른) **coldest** (가장 추운) **most famous** (가장 유명한)	명사	**+**	**in** my class (나의 반에서) **of** the year (일 년 중에)

Ms. Adams is **the best teacher in** my school.
Tony runs **the fastest in** his class.
January is **the coldest month of** the year.
He is **the most famous actor in** Korea.

👅 **My Grammar Notes**

1 비교급: 형용사/부사＋(e)r 또는 more＋형용사/부사
   old → older   beautiful → ＿＿＿＿＿＿   busy → ＿＿＿＿＿＿

2 최상급: 형용사/부사＋(e)st 또는 most＋형용사/부사
   large → ＿＿＿＿＿＿   sad → ＿＿＿＿＿＿   popular → most popular

3 비교급＋＿＿＿＿＿＿: ~보다 더 …한

4 ＿＿＿＿＿＿＋최상급(＋in/of ~): ~에서 가장 …한

Warm-Up

A 비교급과 최상급을 쓰세요. [비교급, 최상급 만들기]

1. long – longer – longest
2. big – bigger –
3. small – – smallest
4. good – – best
5. cheap – cheaper –
6. famous – more famous –
7. tall – –
8. young – –
9. many – –
10. heavy – –
11. fast – –
12. interesting – –
13. large – –
14. bad – –
15. popular – –
16. happy – –
17. expensive – –
18. sad – –

Words

cheap 값이 싼
interesting 흥미로운
expensive (값이) 비싼

B 비교급 문장이면 **O**, 최상급 문장이면 **V** 표시하세요. 〔비교급, 최상급〕

1. My sister is older than you.   **O**

2. I'm the tallest in my family.

3. He sings better than me.

4. This shirt is more expensive than that shirt.

5. He is the most famous soccer player in Korea.

6. Alice is more beautiful than her sister.

7. This is the longest bridge in my country.

8. It was the best day.

C ( ) 안에서 알맞은 것을 고르세요. 〔비교급, 최상급〕

1. The rat is (small / (smaller)) than the cat.

2. This building is the (taller / tallest) in Seoul.

3. My mother is (older / oldest) than my father.

4. It is the (hotter / hottest) day of the year.

5. Health is (importanter / more important) than money.

6. Math is the (easiest / most easiest) subject for me.

7. I have (less / least) money than you.

8. Brandon is the (lazier / laziest) student in the class.

Practice

A 우리말과 같은 뜻이 되도록 주어진 말을 이용하여 빈칸에 알맞은 말을 쓰세요. (최상급 앞에는 **the**를 쓰세요.)

1. 더 높은 산 (high) → **higher** mountain

2. 가장 비싼 음식 (expensive) → ___ food

3. 더 안전한 장소 (safe) → ___ place

4. 가장 행복한 순간 (happy) → ___ moment

5. 가장 부유한 남자 (rich) → ___ man

6. 더 짧은 바지 (short) → ___ pants

7. 더 유명한 가수 (famous) → ___ singer

8. 가장 인기 있는 음료 (popular) → ___ drink

9. 가장 어린 아이 (young) → ___ child

10. 더 느린 동물 (slow) → ___ animal

11. 최고의 방법 (good) → ___ way

12. 가장 긴 강 (long) → ___ river

13. 가장 우스운 농담 (funny) → ___ joke

14. 더 쉬운 질문 (easy) → ___ question

15. 최악의 사고 (bad) → ___ accident

16. 가장 빠른 차 (fast) → ___ car

17. 가장 어려운 문제 (difficult) → ___ problem

18. 가장 흥미로운 영화 (interesting) → ___ movie

B 다음 표를 보고, 주어진 말을 이용하여 문장을 완성하세요.

Words

laptop
노트북 컴퓨터
smartphone
스마트폰

1.   tall / short

이름	Jessica	Yuri	Sunny
키	143cm	147cm	138cm

1) Yuri is   **taller than**   Jessica.

2) Sunny is   Yuri.

3) Yuri is   of the girls.

2.   young / old

이름	Kate	Brian	Henry
나이	2	9	14

1) Brian is   Henry.

2) Henry is   Kate.

3) Kate is   of three.

3.   cheap / expensive

제품	Camera	Laptop	Smartphone
가격	$400	$900	$800

1) The camera is   the laptop.

2) The smartphone is   the camera.

3) The laptop is   of the three.

C 주어진 단어를 알맞은 형태로 바꿔 빈칸에 쓰세요.

Words

Pinocchio 피노키오

nose 코

earth 지구

grade 점수, 성적

friendship 우정

1. **long**
   1) Pinocchio has a __long__ nose.
   2) Pinocchio has a _____ nose than you.

2. **clean**
   1) Most fish live in _____ water.
   2) This fish lives in the _____ water.

3. **sad**
   1) It was a very _____ song.
   2) It was the _____ song on her album.

4. **fast**
   1) Jim runs _____ than me.
   2) Jim is the _____ boy in our class.

5. **beautiful**
   1) This flower is really _____ .
   2) These are the _____ flowers in the garden.

D 밑줄 친 부분을 바르게 고쳐 쓰세요.

1. A car goes <u>slow than</u> a train. → **slower than**

2. The sun is <u>biger than</u> the earth. → _____

3. My parents' room is <u>larger</u> mine. → _____

4. It is <u>most popular</u> song of the year. → _____

5. *Iron Man* is <u>the goodest</u> movie. → _____

6. My English grade was <u>worst than</u> yours. → _____

7. Is friendship <u>more importanter</u> than love? → _____

E 우리말과 같은 뜻이 되도록 주어진 말을 이용하여 문장을 완성하세요.

Words

turtle 거북이
light 가벼운
next 다음의
shop 가게
world 세계
cozy 아늑한

1. Tony는 우리 중 가장 게으르다. (lazy)

→ Tony is ___the laziest___ of us.

2. 토끼는 거북이보다 빠르다. (fast)

→ A rabbit is _____ a turtle.

3. 이 상자는 저 상자보다 가볍다. (light)

→ This box is _____ that box.

4. Sally는 우리 가족 중에서 가장 어리다. (young)

→ Sally is _____ in our family.

5. 오늘은 어제보다 덥다. (hot)

→ Today is _____ yesterday.

6. 이 수학 문제는 다음 문제보다 더 어렵다. (difficult)

→ This math problem is _____ the next one.

7. 이 드레스가 그 가게에서 가장 저렴하다. (cheap)

→ This dress is _____ in the shop.

8. 그의 새 머리 모양은 예전 것보다 낫다. (good)

→ His new hairstyle is _____ his old one.

9. 세계에서 가장 긴 강이 무엇인가요? (long)

→ What is _____ river in the world?

10. 너의 삶에서 가장 중요한 것은 무엇이니? (important)

→ What is _____ thing in your life?

11. 세상에서 집이 제일 아늑한 장소이다. (cozy)

→ Home is _____ place in the world.

A 보기의 단어를 이용하여 우리말에 맞게 문장을 완성하세요.

> 보기 small   high   large   cold

1. 겨울은 가을보다 춥다. (fall)

→ Winter _____ is colder than fall _____.

2. 독도는 제주도보다 작다. (Jeju Island)

→ Dokdo _____.

3. 러시아는 세계에서 가장 큰 나라이다. (country)

→ Russia _____ in the world.

4. 백두산은 한국에서 가장 높은 산이다. (mountain)

→ Mt. Baekdu _____ in Korea.

B 보기와 같이 비교급을 이용하여 두 문장을 한 문장으로 고쳐 쓰세요.

> 보기 I'm 13 years old. Chris is 10 years old.
> ⇨ I'm older than Chris.

1. David is 16 years old. Jason is 14 years old. (young)

→ Jason _____ is younger than David _____.

2. Billy is 157 cm tall. Robert is 165 cm tall. (tall)

→ Robert _____.

3. The box of kiwis weighs 1 kg. The box of pears weighs 2 kg. (heavy)

→ The box of pears _____.

C 우리말과 같은 뜻이 되도록 주어진 말을 바르게 배열하세요.

1. 내 방은 네 방보다 어둡다.

(darker / your room / than / is / my room)

→ _____My room is darker than your room._____

2. 세상에서 가장 부유한 사람은 누구니?

(who / the richest / is / person / in the world)

→ _____

3. 그는 모든 군인 중에서 가장 용감했다.

(all the soldiers / was / of / he / the bravest)

→ _____

4. 오늘은 어제보다 따뜻하다.

(than / warmer / yesterday / is / today)

→ _____

D 다음 대화를 읽고, 밑줄 친 부분을 바르게 고쳐 쓰세요.

A: Mirror, who is ❶ the beautifullest woman in the world?

B: It is Snow White, my queen.

A: Last year, you said I was ❷ the most pretty woman!

B: Yes, I did. But now, she is ❸ more pretty than you!

↓

❶ _____the most beautiful_____   ❷ _____

❸ _____

Words **fall** 가을   **island** 섬   **weigh** 무게가 ~이다   **pear** 배   **person** 사람
soldier 군인   **brave** 용감한   **queen** 여왕

Wrap-Up Test

1. 비교급을 만드는 방법이 나머지와 <u>다른</u> 것을 고르세요.

① long   ② short

③ young   ④ expensive

⑤ tall

2. 비교급과 최상급의 형태가 <u>잘못</u> 짝지어진 것을 고르세요.

① many – more – most

② rich – richer – richest

③ good – worse – worst

④ fat – fatter – fattest

⑤ useful – more useful – most useful

3. 빈칸에 들어갈 수 <u>없는</u> 것을 고르세요.

> Justine is more _____ than me.

① smarter   ② active   ③ popular

④ famous   ⑤ careful

[4-5] 빈칸에 알맞은 말을 고르세요.

4.

> Peter has _____ IQ in his class.

① higher   ② higher than

③ most high   ④ the highest

⑤ more high

5.

> It is the oldest Chinese restaurant _____ this town.

① of   ② in   ③ than

④ the   ⑤ more

6. 우리말을 영어로 바르게 옮긴 것을 고르세요.

> 그것은 오늘 최악의 뉴스였다.

① It was the worst news of the day.

② It was the worse news of the day.

③ It was the bad news in the day.

④ It was the worst news than the day.

⑤ It was the worse news than the day.

Words   **useful** 유용한   **smart** 똑똑한, 영리한   **active** 활동적인, 적극적인   **careful** 조심하는, 주의 깊은   **IQ** 아이큐, 지능지수   **Chinese restaurant** 중국 음식점   **town** 마을

[7-8] 빈칸에 알맞은 말이 바르게 짝지어진 것을 고르세요.

7.

- Alex is a _____ guitar player than me.
- Olivia is the _____ runner in my school.

① good – better ② better – best

③ better – well ④ good – best

⑤ best – better

8.

- Can you come here _____ than he?
- July is the hottest month _____ the year.

① early – in ② early – of

③ earlier – in ④ earlier – of

⑤ earliest – of

9. 다음 내용과 일치하지 <u>않는</u> 것을 고르세요.

> I am 15 years old. Alice is 17 years old.
> Tom is 10 years old.

① Tom is younger than me.

② Alice is older than Tom.

③ I'm older than Alice.

④ Alice is the oldest of the three.

⑤ Tom is the youngest of the three.

10. <u>틀린</u> 문장을 고르세요.

① Your cat is cuter than mine.

② The subway is slower than that train.

③ This box is heavyer than that one.

④ This room is the largest one in this hotel.

⑤ What is the deepest part of the ocean?

Words **player** 선수; 연주자 **cute** 귀여운 **deep** 깊은 **part** 부분 **ocean** 바다, 해양

11. 밑줄 친 부분을 바르게 고친 것을 고르세요.

• She is <u>diligenter</u> than her sister.

• Today is <u>most warm</u> than yesterday.

① diligent – warm

② more diligent – warmer

③ most diligent – the most warm

④ the most diligent – the warmer

⑤ the more diligent – most warmest

12. 우리말과 같은 뜻이 되도록 주어진 단어를 바르게 배열하세요.

나는 반에서 가장 키가 작은 학생이다.

(the shortest / in / student / my class / I'm)

➜ _____

_____

13. 우리말과 같은 뜻이 되도록 빈칸에 알맞은 말을 쓰세요.

My kite is flying _____ _____

yours.

(내 연이 네 것보다 더 높이 날고 있다.)

[14-15] 주어진 단어의 비교급을 이용하여 두 문장의 의미를 한 문장으로 나타내세요.

14.

I get up at 7 o'clock. My brother gets up at 6 o'clock.

➜ I _____ _____ _____

_____ my brother. (late)

15.

Jessie has 3 dollars. Tom has 5 dollars.

➜ Tom has _____ money _____

Jessie. (much)

Words　　**diligent** 부지런한　　**kite** 연　　**fly** 날다　　**dollar** 달러

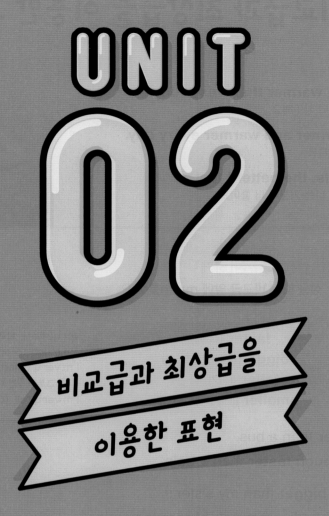

UNIT 02

비교급과 최상급을 이용한 표현

비교급과 최상급을 이용한 표현

Today is much warmer than yesterday.
오늘은 어제보다 훨씬 더 따뜻해요.

It's getting warmer and warmer every day.
날씨가 매일 더 따뜻해져요.

The warmer it is, the better I feel.
날씨가 더 따뜻할수록, 나는 기분이 더 좋아요.

A much + 비교급: 훨씬 더 ~한[하게]

비교급을 강조하고 싶을 때는 비교급 앞에 much를 써요.

much (훨씬)	+	**faster** (더 빠른) **bigger** ((크기가) 더 큰) **taller** ((키가) 더 큰) **smaller** ((크기가) 더 작은)

> very(매우)는 비교급과 함께 쓸 수 없어요.
> I'm **much** taller than him. (O)
> I'm very taller than him. (X)
> (나는 그보다 훨씬 더 커요.)
> I'm **very** tall. (O) (나는 키가 매우 커요.)

A train is **faster** than a bus.
↬ A plane is **much faster** than a train.

My hands are **bigger** than my sister's.
↬ My father's hands are **much bigger** than mine.

B 비교급 + and + 비교급: 점점 더 ~한[하게]

같은 비교급을 and로 연결하면 '점점 더 ~한[하게]'라는 뜻을 나타내요. 짧은 단어(형용사·부사)는 '단어 + -er and 단어 + -er'의 형태로, 긴 단어는 'more and more + 단어'의 형태로 써요.

비교급	and	비교급

I'm getting **taller and taller**.
It is becoming **colder and colder**.
English is becoming **more and more important**.

C the+비교급, the+비교급: ~할수록 점점 더 …하다

문장 맨 앞에 'the+비교급'을 두어 표현할 수 있어요.

> The more, the better.
> The more you get, the more you want.
> The earlier I go to bed, the earlier I get up.
> The bigger the bag is, the more expensive it is.

D one of the+최상급+복수명사: 가장 ~한 …중 하나

> It is one of the nicest rooms in this hotel.
> They are one of the best bands in the world.
> Steve Jobs was one of the most famous CEOs in the world.

🫘 **My Grammar Notes**

1 비교급을 강조할 때는 비교급 앞에 much를 쓴다.
   My fingers are _____ _____ than my friend's.
   (내 손가락은 나의 친구의 것보다 훨씬 길다.)

2 비교급+_____+비교급: 점점 더 ~한

3 _____+비교급, _____+비교급: ~할수록 점점 더 …하다

4 _____ of the+최상급+복수명사: 가장 ~한 …중 하나
   _____ of the tallest buildings in Korea

Warm-Up

A ( ) 안에서 알맞은 것을 고르세요. 〔비교급의 강조〕

1. Eric is ((very)/ much) smart.

2. August is (very / much) hotter than April.

3. My father walks (very / much) fast.

4. China is (very / much) larger than Japan.

5. This sweater is (very / much) nicer than that one.

6. This room is (very / much) clean.

B 우리말과 같은 뜻이 되도록 ( ) 안에서 알맞은 것을 고르세요. 〔비교급 표현〕

1. 빠르면 빠를수록 더 좋다.
   → The sooner, the ((better)/ best).

2. 그녀를 알면 알수록, 나는 그녀가 더 좋아진다.
   → The more I know her, the (more / most) I like her.

3. 네가 가진 돈이 많으면 많을수록, 너는 더 많이 원하게 된다.
   → The more money you have, (more / the more) you want.

4. 점점 더 따뜻해지고 있다.
   → It's getting (warm and warm / warmer and warmer).

5. 그 이야기는 점점 더 흥미로워졌다.
   → The story became more and (more / most) interesting.

6. 내 감기는 점점 더 심해지고 있다.
   → My cold is getting (worst and worst / worse and worse).

C 우리말과 같은 뜻이 되도록 빈칸에 알맞은 말을 쓰세요.

> one of the + 최상급 + 복수명사

1. 서울에서 가장 좋은 식당 중 하나 (good)

   → one of the best   restaurants in Seoul

2. 미국에서 가장 큰 도시 중 하나 (large)

   →   cities in the U.S.

3. 태평양에서 가장 작은 섬 중 하나 (small, island)

   →   in the Pacific

4. 세계에서 가장 유명한 배우 중 하나 (famous, actor)

   →   in the world

5. 나의 인생에서 가장 행복한 순간 중 하나 (happy, moment)

   →   in my life

D 학생들의 100미터 달리기 기록을 보고, 알맞은 것을 고르세요. 비교급, 최상급 표현

Yujin	Sunny	Jinho	Minwoo	Taemin
11.8	17	13	16.5	12

(단위: 초)

1. Jinho ran (faster / slower) than Minwoo.

2. Yujin ran (much fast / much faster) than Sunny.

3. Taemin is one of (the fastest / the slowest) students.

4. Minwoo ran much (faster / slower) than Yujin.

5. Sunny is (the slowest / slower) of them all.

Practice

A 밑줄 친 부분을 강조할 때 **very** 또는 **much**가 들어갈 위치를 표시하고, 빈칸에 알맞은 말을 쓰세요.

1. 1) They moved to a ✓larger house.   much

    2) They live in a <u>large</u> house.

2. 1) Judy plays the piano <u>well</u>.

    2) Judy plays the piano <u>better</u> than me.

3. 1) The cake is <u>sweet</u>.

    2) This chocolate is <u>sweeter</u> than the cake.

4. 1) Olivia's garden is <u>tidy</u>.

    2) Olivia's garden is <u>tidier</u> than mine.

B 우리말과 같은 뜻이 되도록 보기의 단어를 이용하여 빈칸에 알맞은 말을 쓰세요.

보기	fat	popular	dark	good

1. 점점 더 어두워지고 있다.

   → It's getting _____ and _____.

2. 경제가 점점 좋아지고 있다.

   → The economy is _____.

3. 그 개는 점점 더 뚱뚱해지고 있다.

   → The dog is getting _____.

4. 그 밴드는 점점 더 인기를 얻고 있다.

   → The band is getting _____ and _____.

Words

sweet 달콤한
garden 정원
tidy 깔끔한
fat 뚱뚱한
popular
인기 있는
dark 어두운
economy 경제
band
밴드, 악단

C 빈칸에 알맞지 <u>않은</u> 것을 고르세요.

1. The CEO is ~~dangerous~~ busy.

① so   ② much ✓   ③ very   ④ really

2. This car is much _____ than that car.

① faster   ② bigger   ③ expensive   ④ cheaper

3. The trees are _____.

① green   ② tall   ③ very tallest   ④ very tall

4. Jennifer got more and more _____.

① popular   ② happier   ③ beautiful   ④ famous

5. She is one of the _____ people in the world.

① run   ② oldest   ③ most famous   ④ richest

6. He is one of the greatest _____ in history.

① musicians   ② artists   ③ presidents   ④ scientist

Words

CEO (회사의) 최고경영자
history 역사
musician 음악가
artist 예술가
president 대통령
exercise 운동하다
laugh 웃다
strong 튼튼한
become ~이 되다, ~해지다
score 점수
tired 피곤한

D 자연스러운 문장이 되도록 연결하세요.

1. The harder you study, •　　　• ⓐ the more time you'll have.

2. The earlier you get up, •　　　• ⓑ the stronger I became.

3. The more you sleep, •　　　• ⓒ the better score you'll get.

4. The more I exercised, •　　　• ⓓ the less tired you will be.

5. The more we read, •　　　• ⓔ the happier we are.

6. The more we laugh, •　　　• ⓕ the more we learned.

E 보기에서 적절한 말을 이용하여 우리말에 맞게 고쳐 쓰세요.

보기 large   difficult   famous   tall   hot   dangerous

1. 1) There are many   **tall**   buildings in Seoul. (높은)

2) This building is   **much taller**   than the 63 Building.
(훨씬 더 높은)

2. 1) Yuna Kim is a   Korean figure skater. (유명한)

2) She is becoming   . (점점 더 유명한)

3. 1) Elephants are   than bears. (더 큰)

2) The elephant is one of   animals in the
world. (가장 큰)

4. 1) Skiing is sometimes   . (위험한)

2) Snowboarding is   than skiing.
(훨씬 더 위험한)

5. 1) The math test was   . (매우 어려운)

2) The math test was getting   .
(점점 더 어려운)

3) The science test was   than the math
test. (훨씬 더 어려운)

6. 1) Today is one of   days of the year. (가장 더운)

2) It is getting   . (점점 더 더운)

3) This summer is   than last summer.
(훨씬 더 더운)

F 우리말과 같은 뜻이 되도록 주어진 단어를 이용하여 문장을 완성하세요.

Words

weak 약한
signal 신호
comfortable 편안한
ship 배
on earth 지구상에서
angry 화가 난
cute 귀여운
river 강
blue whale 대왕고래
loud (소리가) 큰, 시끄러운

1. Henry는 Josh보다 훨씬 더 영리하다. (smart)

   → Henry is ___much smarter___ than Josh.

2. 그 신호는 점점 더 약해지고 있다. (weak)

   → The signal is getting _____ .

3. Janet은 학교에서 가장 인기 있는 소녀 중 한 명이다. (popular)

   → Janet is one of _____ girls in school.

4. 이 소파는 저 의자보다 훨씬 더 편안하다. (comfortable)

   → This sofa is _____ than that chair.

5. 네가 더 가지게 되면 될수록, 너는 더 원하게 된다. (many)

   → The more you have, _____ you want.

G 밑줄 친 부분을 바르게 고쳐 쓰세요.

1. James is <u>very</u> taller than his friends.   →   ___much___

2. This is <u>one</u> the largest ships on earth.   →   _____

3. He became <u>the more</u> and more angry.   →   _____

4. My dog is <u>much cute</u> than the dog.   →   _____

5. It is one of <u>the longest river</u> in Korea.   →   _____

6. The earlier I get up, <u>the best</u> I feel.   →   _____

7. Blue whales are one of <u>loudest animals</u> in the world.

   →   _____

A 표의 내용에 맞게 주어진 단어를 바르게 배열하세요.

국가명	China	Brazil	India
면적	960	851	328

(단위: 10,000 ㎢)

1. (Brazil / India / than / is / larger)

→ _____ Brazil is larger than India. _____

2. (China / India / much / is / larger / than)

→ _____

3. (India / country / of the three / smallest / is / the)

→ _____

B 우리말과 같은 뜻이 되도록 주어진 말을 이용하여 문장을 완성하세요.

1. 1) 내 카메라는 Julie의 카메라보다 훨씬 더 무겁다. (heavy)

→ My camera is ___much___ ___heavier___ ___than___ Julie's.

2) 이 책은 저 책보다 훨씬 더 두껍다. (thick)

→ _____ This book is much thicker than that book. _____

2. 1) 세계는 점점 더 작아지고 있다. (small)

→ The world is getting _____ _____ _____.

2) 지구가 점점 더 따뜻해지고 있다. (the earth, warm)

→ _____

3. 1) K2는 세계에서 가장 높은 산 중 하나이다. (high)

→ K2 is one of _____ _____ mountains in the world.

2) 고래는 지구상에서 가장 큰 동물 중 하나이다. (a whale, big, animal)

→ _____

4. 1) 이 다리는 저 다리보다 훨씬 오래되었다. (old)

→ This bridge is _____ _____ _____ that bridge.

2) 내 컴퓨터는 너의 컴퓨터보다 훨씬 빠르다. (computer, fast)

→ _____

5. 1) 더 많이 알수록, 나는 더 많이 할 수 있다.

→ _____ _____ I know, _____ _____ I can do.

2) 더 많이 배울수록, 나는 더 많이 잊어버린다. (learn, forget)

→ _____

C 다음 글을 읽고, 밑줄 친 부분을 바르게 고쳐 쓰세요.

I wanted to be a member of the school baseball team, so I started to practice. At first, ❶ harder I practiced, ❷ the worst I got. But I didn't give up. In the end, I became ❸ very better than before. Now, I am one of ❹ best baseball player on my team.

↓

❶ ___the harder I practiced___   ❷ _____

❸ _____   ❹ _____

Words **country** 나라 **thick** 두꺼운 **whale** 고래 **start** 시작하다 **practice** 연습하다
give up 포기하다 **in the end** 마침내 **before** 이전에

Wrap-Up Test

[1-3] 빈칸에 알맞은 것을 고르세요.

1.

> My older brother is _____ stronger than me.

① a   ② much   ③ the

④ very   ⑤ more

2.

> He is one of _____ tennis players in the world.

① good   ② better

③ best   ④ a best

⑤ the best

3.

> _____ you work, the more money you can make.

① Harder   ② Hardest

③ The hard   ④ The harder

⑤ The hardest

4. 빈칸에 알맞은 말이 바르게 짝지어진 것을 고르세요.

> • He is becoming richer and _____.
> • She is one of the _____ designers in Korea.

① richer – famouser

② richer – most famous

③ more rich – famouser

④ more rich – most famous

⑤ rich – most famous

5. 빈칸에 공통으로 알맞은 것을 고르세요.

> • You have to be _____ careful.
> • These days _____ and _____ people are reading blogs.

① the   ② many

③ more   ④ much

⑤ the more

Words   **make money** 돈을 벌다   **designer** 디자이너   **careful** 조심성 있는   **blog** 블로그

6. 밑줄 친 부분을 바르게 고친 것을 고르세요.

> • This building is <u>very</u> taller than our house.
> • The hungrier you are, <u>more</u> you eat.

① most – much
② much – much
③ more – many
④ more – the more
⑤ much – the more

7. 우리말과 같은 뜻이 되도록 빈칸에 알맞은 말을 쓰세요.

> The days are getting _____ _____ _____.
> (낮이 점점 더 짧아지고 있다.)

8. 틀린 문장을 고르세요.

① It's getting dark and dark.
② My cat is bigger than my dog.
③ Her voice is very beautiful.
④ This flower is much prettier than that flower.
⑤ The more you read, the wiser you become.

[9-10] 우리말을 영어로 바르게 옮긴 것을 고르세요.

9.

> 더 많이 웃을수록, 너는 더 행복해질 것이다.

① More you smile, happier you will be.
② You smile and smile, you will be happy.
③ The more you smile, happier you will be.
④ The more you smile, you will be happy.
⑤ The more you smile, the happier you will be.

10.

> 그는 우리나라에서 가장 빠른 달리기 선수 중 한 사람이다.

① He is one of the fast runners in our country.
② He is one of the fastest runner in our country.
③ He is one of the faster runners in our country.
④ He is one of the fastest runners in our country.
⑤ He is one of the faster runner than our country.

Words   **hungry** 배고픈   **day** 낮, 하루   **voice** 목소리   **wise** 현명한   **smile** 웃다

11. 빈칸에 than이 들어갈 수 없는 것을 고르세요.

① I'm much older _____ you.

② I like apples more _____ bananas.

③ This test is more important _____ the next one.

④ She's one of the busiest people _____ the company.

⑤ He works harder _____ the other men in our group.

12. 빈칸에 비교급이 들어갈 수 없는 것을 고르세요.

① It is getting hotter and _____.

② The more I practice cooking, the _____ I like it.

③ My uncle bought me a very _____ bag.

④ My feet are much _____ than yours.

⑤ She ate _____ cookies than my brother.

서술형
13. 우리말과 같은 뜻이 되도록 주어진 말을 이용하여 문장을 완성하세요.

침팬지는 원숭이보다 훨씬 더 영리하다. (smart)

→ Chimpanzees are _____

_____ monkeys.

서술형
14. 틀린 부분을 찾아 바르게 고쳐 쓰세요.

The faster the train runs, you can get there earlier.

→ _____

_____

서술형
15. 주어진 단어를 바르게 배열하여 문장을 완성하세요.

successful / one / she / actresses / most / the / of / is

→ _____

_____

in Korea.

Words foot 발 (복수형 feet) chimpanzee 침팬지 monkey 원숭이 successful 성공한
actress (여자) 배우

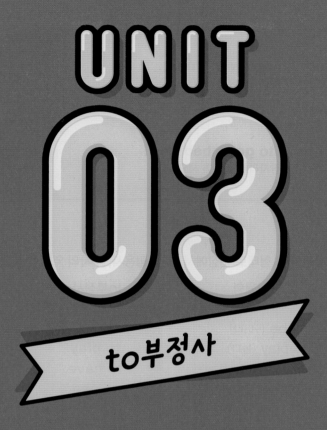

UNIT 03

to부정사

> **I plan to go hiking tomorrow morning.**
> 나는 내일 아침에 도보 여행을 갈 계획이에요.
>
> **I'll bring some water to drink.**
> 나는 마실 물을 조금 가져갈 거예요.
>
> **To get up early, I have to go to bed now.**
> 일찍 일어나기 위해서, 나는 지금 잠자리에 들어야 해요.

A to부정사의 형태

to부정사는 'to+동사원형'의 형태로 문장에서 명사, 형용사, 부사의 역할을 해요.

	동사원형		to부정사
to	+	be (~이다) play (놀다) have (가지다) see (보다)	→	to be to play to have to see

> to 뒤에는 항상 동사원형을 쓰는 것에 주의해야 해요.
> to plays (X)
> to played (X)

B 명사처럼 쓰이는 to부정사: ~하기, ~하는 것 참고 Unit 04

to부정사는 명사처럼 문장에서 be동사나 일반동사 뒤에 쓸 수 있어요.

주어	+	be (~이다) want (원하다) hope (바라다) plan (계획하다) decide (결심하다) like (좋아하다) learn (배우다) wish (소망하다)	+	to부정사

My dream **is to be** a singer.

I **want to take** a break.

We **hope to see** you again.

He **decided to lose** weight.

We **planned to travel** to India on foot.

The scientist **likes to create** monsters.

> 동사 뒤에는 명사 또는 명사처럼 쓰이는 to부정사를 써요.
> 동사 뒤에 바로 동사를 쓸 수는 없어요.
> I want a car. (O) (나는 차를 원해요.)
> I want to buy a car. (O) (나는 차를 사고 싶어요.)
> I want buy a car. (X)

C 형용사처럼 쓰이는 to부정사: ~할

to부정사는 형용사처럼 명사나 대명사를 꾸며줄 수 있어요.
하지만, to부정사는 형용사와 달리 (대)명사의 뒤에서 꾸며줘요.

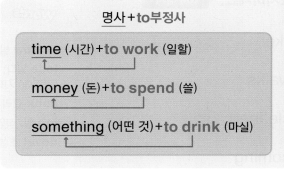

명사+to부정사

time (시간)+**to work** (일할)

money (돈)+**to spend** (쓸)

something (어떤 것)+**to drink** (마실)

It's time **to work**.

I have no money **to spend**.

Do you want something **to drink**?

She has a lot of work **to do**.

D 부사처럼 쓰이는 to부정사: ~하기 위해, ~하려고

to부정사는 부사처럼 '~하기 위해, ~하려고'의 의미로 목적을 나타낼 수 있어요.

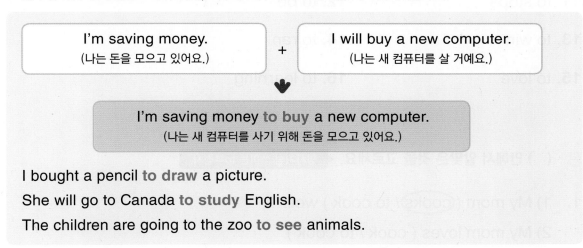

I'm saving money.
(나는 돈을 모으고 있어요.)

+

I will buy a new computer.
(나는 새 컴퓨터를 살 거예요.)

⬇

I'm saving money **to buy** a new computer.
(나는 새 컴퓨터를 사기 위해 돈을 모으고 있어요.)

I bought a pencil **to draw** a picture.

She will go to Canada **to study** English.

The children are going to the zoo **to see** animals.

🫘 My Grammar Notes

1 to부정사 = _____+동사원형

2 _____처럼 쓰이는 to부정사: ~하는 것, ~하기

   I want _____ drink some water. (나는 물을 마시고 싶어.)

3 _____처럼 쓰이는 to부정사: ~할, ~하는

   I want some water _____ drink. (나는 마실 물을 원해.)

4 _____처럼 쓰이는 to부정사: ~하기 위해, ~하려고

   I went to the kitchen _____ drink some water. (난 물을 마시러 부엌에 갔다.)

A to부정사의 형태가 맞으면 O, 틀리면 X 표시하세요. ◄ to부정사

1. to start   O
2. to like
3. to goes
4. to walks
5. to borrow
6. to cleaned
7. to wanted
8. to coming
9. to lose
10. to do
11. to stops
12. to be
13. to win
14. to ran
15. to love
16. to learning

Words

borrow 빌리다
lose 잃다;
(경기에) 지다
cook 요리하다
job 일; 직업
novel 소설

B ( ) 안에서 알맞은 것을 고르세요. ◄ 명사처럼 쓰이는 to부정사

1. 1) My mom (cooks / to cook) well.
   2) My mom loves (cook / to cook).

2. 1) Her dog likes (to eat / eat).
   2) Her dog (eats / to eat) a lot.

3. 1) I want (to listen / listen) to some music.
   2) I usually (listen / to listen) to the radio at night.

4. 1) I (got / to get) a new job a month ago.
   2) She decided (get / to get) a job.

5. 1) I started (read / to read) this novel yesterday.
   2) I will (read / to read) that novel this weekend.

C **to부정사에 O 표시하고, to부정사가 꾸며주는 말에 밑줄을 그으세요.**

◀ 형용사처럼 쓰이는 to부정사

1. There is a lot of <u>laundry</u> (to do)

2. Billy has work to do tonight.

3. We have plans to go hiking.

4. Now is the time to learn English.

5. There is nothing to eat in the refrigerator.

6. Paul bought some newspapers to read.

7. My sister doesn't have any clothes to wear.

Words

laundry
빨래, 빨랫감
work 일
tonight 오늘밤
plan
계획하다; 계획
refrigerator
냉장고
clothes 옷
wear
입다, 착용하다
on time
제시간에
catch 잡다
hurry 서두르다
station 역
stadium
경기장
visa 비자

D **빈칸에 들어갈 알맞은 말을 보기에서 골라 쓰세요.** ◀ 부사처럼 쓰이는 to부정사

보기	to be on time	to take pictures
	to catch the train	to visit Canada
	to buy some food	to see a baseball game

1. Patrick hurried   **to be on time**   .

2. She ran to the station _____ .

3. He visited the stadium _____ .

4. Do I need a visa _____ ?

5. She went shopping _____ .

6. Most people use a smartphone _____ .

Practice

A to가 들어갈 위치에 V 표시한 후, 우리말로 해석하세요.

1. He likes ✓swim a lot. → 그는 수영하는 것을 매우 좋아한다.

2. It's time say goodbye. →

3. She came see me yesterday. →

4. He decided be a scientist. →

5. It's your turn do the dishes. →

6. I went to the bakery buy some bread.

   →

B 우리말과 같은 뜻이 되도록 주어진 단어를 이용하여 문장을 완성하세요.

1. 나는 그 영화를 다시 보기를 원한다. (see)

   → I want   to see   the movie again.

2. 그는 정시에 도착하기 위해 택시를 탔다. (arrive)

   → He took a taxi   on time.

3. Jane은 일찍 일어나려고 알람을 맞췄다. (wake up)

   → Jane set the alarm   early.

4. Sam은 시험에 합격하기 위해 열심히 공부했다. (pass)

   → Sam studied hard   the test.

5. 나는 언젠가 아프리카에 가보길 희망한다. (visit)

   → I hope   Africa someday.

6. 그녀는 자신의 차를 고쳐줄 사람을 찾고 있다. (fix)

   → She is looking for someone   her car.

Words

say goodbye 작별 인사를 하다

scientist 과학자

turn 차례, 순번

do the dishes 설거지하다

bakery 제과점

arrive 도착하다

set an alarm 알람을 맞추다

pass (시험에) 합격하다

Africa 아프리카

fix 수리하다

look for ~를 찾다

C 밑줄 친 **to부정사**의 의미로 알맞은 것을 보기에서 골라 기호를 쓰세요.

Words

professor 교수
move 옮기다;
이사하다
regularly
규칙적으로
suddenly
갑자기
save
모으다; 구하다
taekwondo
태권도
earth 지구
hairdresser's
미용실
get a haircut
머리를 자르다,
이발하다
wish 소원

보기   ⓐ ~하는 것, ~하기   ⓑ ~할   ⓒ ~하기 위해, ~하려고

1. I want <u>to be</u> a professor.   ⓐ

2. There are lots of boxes <u>to move</u>.

3. Please give me something <u>to drink</u>.

4. You need <u>to exercise</u> regularly.

5. Suddenly, it started <u>to rain</u>.

6. I saved money <u>to buy</u> a new computer.

7. I have no time <u>to read</u> books.

8. Jennifer wants <u>to learn</u> taekwondo.

9. My grandparents came here <u>to see</u> me.

10. He got up early <u>to go</u> to the mountains.

11. My father likes <u>to play</u> tennis.

12. She went to France <u>to study</u> fashion design.

13. I bought a dress <u>to wear</u> on my birthday.

14. What can we do <u>to save</u> the earth?

15. He went to the hairdresser's <u>to get</u> a haircut.

16. Is there anyone <u>to help</u> me?

17. My wish is <u>to be</u> stronger than everyone.

18. Brad is looking in his bag <u>to find</u> his key.

D 우리말과 같은 뜻이 되도록 주어진 단어를 이용하여 문장을 완성하세요.

Words

keep a diary
일기를 쓰다

marry
결혼하다

Would you like ~?
~하시겠어요?

magazine
잡지

expect
예상하다, 기대하다

1. 그는 일기를 쓰기로 결심했다. (decide, keep)

   ➔ He   **decided to keep**   a diary.

2. 너는 수영하는 것을 언제 배웠니? (learn, swim)

   ➔ When did you   ?

3. 그는 그녀와 결혼하기를 원했다. (want, marry)

   ➔ He   her.

4. 나는 내 방을 청소하기 시작했다. (begin, clean)

   ➔ I   my room.

5. 마실 것 좀 드릴까요? (something, drink)

   ➔ Would you like   ?

6. 나는 운동할 시간이 없다. (time, exercise)

   ➔ I don't have   .

7. 나는 너에게 말할 것이 없다. (nothing, say)

   ➔ I have   to you.

8. 민수는 버스를 탈 돈이 없다. (money, take)

   ➔ Minsu doesn't have   a bus.

9. 그녀는 비행기에서 읽을 잡지가 있다. (a magazine, read)

   ➔ She has   on the plane.

10. 나는 그로부터 좋은 소식을 듣기를 기대한다. (expect, hear)

    ➔ I   good news from him.

E 보기와 같이 두 문장을 연결하여 한 문장으로 쓰세요.

> 보기 I went to the bookstore. I wanted to buy a book.
> ⇨ I went to the bookstore to buy a book.

1. He came to the restaurant. He wanted to eat dinner.
   → He came to the restaurant to eat dinner.

2. We used the map. We wanted to find the hotel.
   → _____

3. I am going to the library. I want to study for my exam.
   → _____

4. She went to the bathroom. She wanted to wash her hands.
   → _____

5. She turned on the computer. She wanted to play games.
   → _____

F 밑줄 친 부분을 바르게 고쳐 쓰세요.

1. I want <u>know</u> the girl's name.   → to know

2. She came here <u>to meeting</u> my brother.   →

3. Jack needs a room <u>to staying</u> in tonight. →

4. My plan is <u>travel</u> around the world.   →

5. We hoped <u>to saw</u> the movie soon.   →

6. Ben took a vacation <u>to visits</u> Europe. →

7. Alex often goes to the park <u>to walks</u> his dog. →

bookstore
서점
map 지도
library 도서관
exam 시험
bathroom
욕실, 화장실
turn on
(전원을) 켜다
travel around the world
세계 여행을 하다
take a vacation
휴가를 얻다
walk a dog
개를 산책시키다

A 우리말과 같은 뜻이 되도록 보기에서 알맞은 말을 골라 문장을 만드세요.

> 보기
> buy a new car   move to another city
> make foreign friends   translate foreign languages

1. 나는 외국인 친구를 사귀고 싶다. (hope)

→ _____ I hope to make foreign friends. _____

2. Andy는 새 차를 살 계획이다. (plan)

→ _____

3. 내 직업은 외국어를 번역하는 것이다. (job)

→ _____

4. 우리는 다른 도시로 이사하기로 결심했다. (decide)

→ _____

B 우리말과 같은 뜻이 되도록 주어진 말을 이용하여 문장을 만드세요.

1. 1) 나는 살을 빼기 위해 운동하고 있다. (lose weight)

→ I'm exercising ____ to lose weight ____.

2) Peter는 자전거를 사기 위해 저축하고 있다. (save, buy a bicycle)

→ ____ Peter is saving to buy a bicycle. ____

2. 1) 민호는 일본어를 배우기 위해 일본에 갔다. (learn Japanese)

→ Minho went to Japan _____.

2) Mia는 뮤지컬을 보기 위해 뉴욕에 갔다. (New York, see musicals)

→ _____

3. 1) 나는 컴퓨터를 고쳐줄 사람을 찾고 있다. (fix my computer)

→ I am looking for someone _____.

2) 그들은 차를 고쳐줄 사람을 기다리고 있다. (wait for, fix their car)

→ _____.

4. 1) Judy는 종종 친구들을 만나러 시내에 간다. (meet her friends)

→ Judy often goes downtown _____.

2) Brian은 종종 낮잠을 자러 집에 간다. (home, take a nap)

→ _____.

C 보기의 단어를 이용하여 빈칸에 알맞은 말을 쓰고 우리말로 해석하세요.

보기	win	be	play	help	get	kick

I love _**to play**_ soccer. Someday, I want _____
a great soccer player. My dream is _____ the
World Cup. But I'm just a beginner right now. I need a
coach _____ me. I'll learn _____ the ball
_____ a goal!

↓

나는 축구하는 것을 정말 좋아해요.

_____

_____

Words   **another** 또 다른   **foreign** 외국의   **translate** 번역하다   **language** 언어
lose weight 살을 빼다   **go downtown** 시내에 가다   **take a nap** 낮잠을 자다
kick (공을) 차다   **beginner** 초보자   **coach** 감독, 코치   **get a goal** 골을 넣다

Wrap-Up Test

[1-2] 빈칸에 알맞은 말을 고르세요.

1.

> I hope _____ you again.

① see   ② saw   ③ seeing

④ to see   ⑤ will see

2.

> We will go to the playground _____ a drone.

① fly   ② flied   ③ flying

④ to fly   ⑤ will fly

[3-4] 빈칸에 들어갈 수 <u>없는</u> 것을 고르세요.

3.

> Sarah decided to _____.

① exercise   ② be a teacher

③ buy a hat   ④ saved money

⑤ go camping

4.

> I want _____.

① eat pizza   ② a new computer

③ to be a pilot   ④ to see her again

⑤ some coffee

5. 빈칸에 알맞은 말이 바르게 짝지어진 것을 고르세요.

> • We take that class _____ English.
> • They wish _____ a dog.

① learn – own   ② learning – own

③ learn – to own   ④ to learn – owning

⑤ to learn – to own

6. 밑줄 친 부분을 바르게 고친 것을 고르세요.

> • She plans to <u>studies</u> abroad.
> • He wore a jacket <u>to is</u> warm.

① studies – is   ② to study – is

③ study – to be   ④ studies – to be

⑤ to study – to be

Words **playground** 놀이터   **drone** 드론   **go camping** 캠핑하러 가다   **pilot** 조종사, 비행사
own 소유하다   **abroad** 해외에서, 해외로   **jacket** 재킷

[7-8] 밑줄 친 **to**부정사의 쓰임이 보기와 다른 것을 고르세요.

7.

I love to go to the movies.

① I like to play soccer.

② We need to finish it today.

③ My father plans to buy a new car.

④ It's time to watch the music show.

⑤ She needs to take a shower.

8.

He ran fast to catch the taxi.

① I met Kate to borrow a book.

② The baby began to cry.

③ She called me to ask a question.

④ We went shopping to buy some clothes.

⑤ We went to the restaurant to have lunch.

[9-10] 우리말을 영어로 바르게 옮긴 것을 고르세요.

9.

너는 이번 일요일에 뭘 하고 싶니?

① What do you want doing this Sunday?

② What are you want to do this Sunday?

③ What do you want do this Sunday?

④ What do you want to do this Sunday?

⑤ What do you want did this Sunday?

10.

Jeff는 먹을 것을 사기 위해 슈퍼마켓에 갔다.

① Jeff went to the supermarket buy some food.

② Jeff went to the supermarket buying some food.

③ Jeff went to the supermarket to buy some food.

④ Jeff went to the supermarket and buy some food.

⑤ Jeff went to the supermarket and bought some food.

Words　　**take a shower** 샤워하다　　**supermarket** 슈퍼마켓

11. 틀린 문장을 고르세요.

① I like to go swimming.

② We need a knife to cut the fruit.

③ They didn't want to lose the game.

④ She has much homework do.

⑤ He raised his hand to ask a question.

서술형

12. 주어진 단어를 이용하여 질문에 알맞은 대답을 완성하세요.

> A: Why are you washing those apples?
>
> B: We are washing the apples _____
>
> _____ apple jam. (make)

서술형

13. 우리말과 같은 뜻이 되도록 주어진 말을 이용하여 문장을 완성하세요.

> 에베레스트산을 오른 최초의 사람은 누구였니?
>
> (the first person, climb Mt. Everest)

→ _____

_____

서술형

14. 우리말과 같은 뜻이 되도록 주어진 말을 바르게 배열하세요.

> 나의 계획은 그곳에 일찍 도착하는 것이다.
>
> (is / my plan / get there / to / early)

→ _____

_____

서술형

15. 우리말과 같은 뜻이 되도록 틀린 부분을 찾아 바르게 고쳐 쓰세요.

> I study hard be a teacher.
>
> (나는 선생님이 되기 위해 열심히 공부한다.)

→ _____

_____

 Words   knife 칼   cut 자르다   **ask a question** 질문하다   **first** 처음의, 최초의

person 사람   **climb** 오르다, 등반하다   **Mt.** 산 (= mountain의 줄임말)

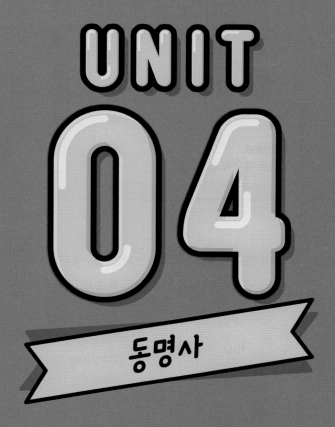

UNIT 04

동명사

🫘 **Vocab Check!** 이번 과에서 배울 단어의 뜻을 확인하고, 모르는 단어에 체크 표시하세요.

✓ **1** naturally — 伸 자연스럽게
2 difficult — 형 어려운
3 health — 명 건강
4 believe — 동 믿다
5 report — 명 보고서
6 carefully — 伸 조심스럽게
7 avoid — 동 피하다
8 habit — 명 습관
9 protect — 동 보호하다
10 quit — 동 그만두다

11 recycle — 동 재활용하다
12 garbage — 명 쓰레기
13 promise — 동 약속하다
14 hate — 동 싫어하다
15 job — 명 일, 직업
16 loudly — 伸 큰 소리로
17 count — 동 (숫자를) 세다
18 water — 명 물 동 물을 주다
19 collect — 동 수집하다
20 office — 명 사무실

21 experience — 명 경험
22 fall asleep — 잠들다
23 photograph — 명 사진
24 environment — 명 환경
25 chopsticks — 명 젓가락
26 newspaper — 명 신문
27 relax — 동 쉬다
28 wild animal — 야생 동물
29 deliver — 동 배달하다
30 persuade — 동 설득하다

04 동명사

Ronda and I enjoy skating.
론다와 나는 스케이트 타는 것을 즐겨요.

Skating is our hobby.
스케이트 타는 것은 우리의 취미예요.

We like skating **on the lake.**
우리는 호수 위에서 스케이트 타는 것을 좋아해요.

 동명사의 형태

동명사는 동사 뒤에 -ing를 붙여 명사처럼 쓰는 말로, '~하는 것, ~하기'로 해석해요.

동사원형 (~하다)

| eat (먹다) |
| take (가지고 가다) |
| play (놀다) |
| see (보다) |

\+ ing ➡

동명사 (~하는 것)

| eating (먹는 것) |
| taking (가지고 가는 것) |
| playing (노는 것) |
| seeing (보는 것) |

B **동명사의 쓰임**

동명사는 명사처럼 문장에서 주어로 쓰이거나 동사 뒤에 목적어로 쓸 수 있어요.

1. 주어로 쓰이는 동명사

동명사는 문장의 맨 앞, 주어 자리에 쓸 수 있어요. 이때 동명사는 to부정사처럼 단수 취급해요.

Swimming
(수영하는 것은)
Playing cards
(카드놀이를 하는 것은)

\+

is fun.
(재미있어요.)

2. 동사 뒤에 쓰이는 동명사

동명사는 be동사나 일반동사 뒤에 쓸 수 있어요.

I enjoy
(나는 즐겨요)

\+

singing. (노래하는 것을)
playing soccer. (축구를 하는 것을)
listening to music. (음악을 듣는 것을)

His job is **teaching** English.

She enjoys **dancing**.

We finished **doing** our homework.

C to부정사와 동명사

뒤에 목적어가 필요한 일반동사 중에는 목적어로 to부정사를 쓰는 동사와 동명사를 쓰는 동사가 있어요.
이 두 가지 종류의 동사를 구분해서 알아두어야 해요.

to부정사만 목적어로 취하는 동사	want (원하다), hope (희망하다), decide (결심하다), wish (바라다), promise (약속하다)
동명사만 목적어로 취하는 동사	enjoy (즐기다), finish (끝내다), keep (계속하다), give up (포기하다), stop (중단하다), quit (그만두다), avoid (피하다)
둘 다 목적어로 취하는 동사	begin (시작하다), start (시작하다), like (좋아하다), love (사랑하다), hate (싫어하다)

I **want to be** a pilot.

We **decided to sell** our house.

They **enjoy watching** musicals.

Did you **finish writing** the letter?

Jenny **likes to sing** songs. = Jenny **likes singing** songs.

🍌 My Grammar Notes

1 동명사: 동사원형+_____

2 동명사는 '~하기, ~하는 것'이라는 의미로 문장에서 _____처럼 쓰인다.

3 동명사가 문장의 주어일 때는 항상 단수 취급한다.
  Smoking _____ bad for your health. (담배를 피우는 것은 당신의 건강에 해로워요.)

4 동사 중에는 목적어로 to부정사를 쓰는 것과 동명사를 쓰는 것이 있다.
  (1) want, decide, hope+_____
  (2) enjoy, finish+_____

5 like, love, start와 같은 동사 뒤에는 to부정사와 동명사 모두 쓸 수 있다.

A 다음 문장에서 동명사를 찾아 **O** 표시하세요. ◀ 동명사의 형태

1. He enjoys (reading) fantasy novels.

2. I like playing computer games.

3. Seeing is believing.

4. My hobby is listening to music.

5. Speaking English naturally is difficult.

6. Eating too much is not good for our health.

7. Keeping a diary is not easy.

8. She finished writing her report.

B ( ) 안에서 알맞은 것을 고르세요. ◀ 동명사의 쓰임

1. 1) I like (watch / (watching)) TV.

   2) I often (watch / watching) movies on Saturday.

2. 1) He doesn't (tell / telling) lies.

   2) He enjoys (tell / telling) funny stories.

3. 1) She (dances / dancing) very well.

   2) She loves (dances / dancing) at parties.

4. 1) My dad (drives / driving) carefully.

   2) My dad avoids (drives / driving) at night.

5. 1) Jenny stopped (playing / plays) the violin.

   2) Jenny (plays / playing) the cello these days.

Words

fantasy
novel
판타지 소설
believe 믿다
hobby 취미
naturally
자연스럽게
health 건강
keep a diary
일기를 쓰다
report 보고서
tell a lie
거짓말하다
funny 재미있는
story 이야기
(복수형
stories)
carefully
조심스럽게
at night 밤에

C 자연스러운 문장이 되도록 연결하세요. 〈 동명사의 쓰임

Words

comic book
만화책

habit 습관

quit 그만두다
(과거형 **quit**)

recycle
재활용하다

garbage
쓰레기

gold medal
금메달

**the Olympic
Games**
올림픽 대회

**bite one's
nails**
손톱을 물어뜯다

protect
보호하다

environment
환경

take a walk
산책하다

job 일, 직업

**brush one's
teeth** 양치하다

shop
사다, 쇼핑하다

1. Reading comic books •   • ⓐ is taking pictures.

2. His new hobby •   • ⓑ is fun.

3. Becoming a singer •   • ⓒ playing the piano.

4. My bad habit •   • ⓓ is biting my nails.

5. Jessica enjoys •   • ⓔ is my dream.

6. My uncle quit •   • ⓕ is not easy.

7. Recycling garbage •   • ⓖ smoking last week.

8. Getting a gold medal •   • ⓗ protects the environment.
   in the Olympic Games

D ( ) 안에서 알맞은 것을 <u>모두</u> 고르세요. 〈 to부정사와 동명사

1. He kept ((talking) / to talk) to me.

2. I don't want (going / to go) there.

3. Tony likes (taking / to take) a walk.

4. She decided (getting / to get) a job.

5. We promised (meeting / to meet) again.

6. Danny hates (brushing / to brush) his teeth.

7. Jenny began (playing / to play) the violin.

8. Kate loves (shopping / to shop) with her friends.

Practice

A 밑줄 친 부분이 동명사로 쓰인 문장에 **V** 표시하세요.

1. Grace loves <u>listening</u> to music.   V

2. My brother is <u>jumping</u> on the bed.

3. Kevin likes <u>talking</u> on the phone.

4. They are <u>laughing</u> loudly.

5. Jessie is <u>sleeping</u> on the sofa.

6. It kept <u>raining</u> for two days.

7. Mrs. Lee is <u>watering</u> her flowers.

8. My little brother started <u>counting</u> to ten.

B ( ) 안에서 알맞은 것을 고르세요.

1. I finished (wash / (washing)) the dishes.

2. Collecting postcards (is / are) her hobby.

3. Minho likes (walks / walking) with his dog.

4. Suddenly, the dog started (bark / barking).

5. Jogging (is / are) good for your health.

6. Why do you keep (watching / to watch) me?

7. Do you like (play / playing) football?

8. Living abroad (is / does) a great experience.

C 보기의 단어를 이용하여 빈칸에 알맞은 동명사를 쓰세요.

보기   learn   exercise   eat   read   play   travel

1. I hate   eating   fish.

2. _____ Spanish is not easy.

3. My dad enjoys _____ golf.

4. Jane finished _____ the book.

5. _____ the world is my dream.

6. _____ regularly keeps you in shape.

D 우리말과 같은 뜻이 되도록 주어진 말을 이용하여 문장을 완성하세요.

1. 산을 오르는 것은 때때로 위험하다. (climb mountains)

   → ___Climbing mountains___ is sometimes dangerous.

2. Cathy는 말 타는 것을 즐기지 않는다. (ride horses)

   → Cathy doesn't enjoy _____.

3. 나의 직업은 사진을 찍는 것이다. (take photographs)

   → My job is _____.

4. 너는 한 시간 동안 계속 달릴 수 있니? (run for an hour)

   → Can you keep _____?

5. 그 학생들은 축구하기를 끝냈니? (play soccer)

   → Did the students finish _____?

6. 내 할아버지는 담배 피우는 것을 피하신다. (smoke cigarettes)

   → My grandfather avoids _____.

Words

exercise 운동하다
travel 여행하다
fish 생선
(복수형 **fish**)
Spanish 스페인어
golf 골프
keep in shape 건강을 유지하다
climb 오르다
dangerous 위험한
photograph 사진
smoke cigarettes 담배를 피우다

E 보기의 단어를 이용하여 문장을 완성하세요.

보기 watch   meet   stay   speak   be   bark   cook   eat

1. I avoid   eating   fast food.

2. Daniel enjoys   horror movies.

3. I hope   my friend in London.

4. The dog kept   at me.

5. Jihun wants   a famous singer.

6. Mom promised   bulgogi for dinner.

7. Please stop   and listen to me.

8. Jane finally decided   in Canada.

F 밑줄 친 부분을 바르게 고쳐 쓰세요.

1. I hope <u>seeing</u> you again. →   to see

2. My dad gave up <u>fix</u> the car. →

3. Using chopsticks <u>aren't</u> easy. →

4. Did you finish <u>read</u> the newspaper? →

5. Jessica wanted <u>speaking</u> English well. →

6. The baby stopped <u>cry</u> and fell asleep. →

7. Bill enjoys <u>to make</u> cookies for his children. →

8. Fans kept <u>to wait</u> outside to see the band. →

G 우리말과 같은 뜻이 되도록 주어진 말을 이용하여 문장을 완성하세요.

Words

relax 쉬다
expect 기대하다, 예상하다

1. 나는 여기에 머무르고 싶다. (want, stay)

   ➔ I _____ want to stay _____ here.

2. Amy는 나에게 계속 전화했다. (keep, call)

   ➔ Amy _____ me.

3. 나는 비행기 조종사가 되고 싶다. (hope, be)

   ➔ I _____ a pilot.

4. 아빠는 담배 피우는 것을 그만두셨다. (stop, smoke)

   ➔ My dad _____ .

5. Mark는 아침 식사 만드는 것을 끝냈다. (finish, make)

   ➔ Mark _____ breakfast.

6. 나는 소파에서 쉬는 것을 즐긴다. (enjoy, relax)

   ➔ I _____ on the sofa.

7. Tom은 스페인어를 배우기로 결정했다. (decide, learn)

   ➔ Tom _____ Spanish.

8. 그는 그녀를 다시 보기를 기대했다. (expect, see)

   ➔ He _____ her again.

9. Mike는 컴퓨터를 고치는 것을 포기했다. (give up, fix)

   ➔ Mike _____ the computer.

10. 엄마는 너무 많이 드시는 것을 피하신다. (avoid, eat)

   ➔ My mom _____ too much.

A 우리말과 같은 뜻이 되도록 보기에서 알맞은 말을 골라 문장을 만드세요.

> 보기   get up early   wear a tie   drive in the rain
>   learn a new language   become a famous actress

1. 새로운 언어를 배우는 것은 재미있다. (interesting)

   → ___Learning a new language is interesting.___

2. 빗속에서 운전하는 것은 안전하지 않다. (not safe)

   → _____

3. 유명한 배우가 되는 것이 그녀의 꿈이다. (her dream)

   → _____

4. 일찍 일어나는 것은 좋은 습관이다. (a good habit)

   → _____

5. 넥타이를 매는 것은 건강에 좋지 않다. (not healthy)

   → _____

B 우리말과 같은 뜻이 되도록 주어진 말을 이용하여 문장을 완성하세요.

1. 1) 나는 새 휴대전화 사는 것을 포기했다. (buy)

      → I gave up ____buying____ a new cell phone.

   2) 우리는 John을 기다리는 것을 포기했다. (wait for)

      → ____We gave up waiting for John.____

2. 1) 그 소년은 나에게 계속 미소를 지었다. (smile)

      → The boy kept _____ at me.

2) Jane은 같은 질문을 계속했다. (ask the same question)

→ _____

3. 1) 나는 숙제하는 것을 마쳤다. (do)

→ I finished _____ my homework.

2) 그는 Jake에게 편지 쓰는 것을 마쳤다. (write a letter to Jake)

→ _____

4. 1) 그는 밤늦게 TV 보는 것을 피한다. (watch)

→ He avoids _____ TV late at night.

2) 나는 밤늦게 치킨 먹는 것을 피한다. (eat chicken)

→ _____

C 다음 대화를 읽고, 밑줄 친 부분을 바르게 고쳐 쓰세요.

My dream ❶ is travel around the world. I went to Europe and the U.S. with my parents. I ❷ hope visiting Africa someday. I like to see wild animals with my own eyes. For this dream, I ❸ started save money. ❹ Do you want join me?

↓

❶ _____ is traveling _____

❷ _____

❸ _____

❹ _____

Words　tie 넥타이　language 언어　actress (여자) 배우　habit 습관　healthy 건강에 좋은
Africa 아프리카　wild animal 야생 동물　own 자신의

Wrap-Up Test

[1-2] 빈칸에 알맞은 말을 고르세요.

1.

> _____ many books is good for students.

① Read ② Reading ③ To reads
④ Reads ⑤ To reading

2.

> I _____ writing a letter.

① decided ② finished ③ wanted
④ hoped ⑤ promised

[3-4] 빈칸에 들어갈 수 <u>없는</u> 것을 고르세요.

3.

> They didn't _____ to do the work.

① like ② plan ③ want
④ enjoy ⑤ hate

4.

> Making snowmen _____.

① isn't difficult ② are fun
③ wasn't easy ④ was exciting
⑤ is interesting

[5-6] 밑줄 친 부분의 쓰임이 <u>다른</u> 것을 고르세요.

5.

① She loves <u>eating</u> fruit.
② I like <u>traveling</u> by train.
③ He is <u>walking</u> on the street.
④ They avoid <u>going</u> out at night.
⑤ We enjoyed <u>shopping</u> at the market.

6.

① Kevin is <u>cleaning</u> his room.
② My sister is <u>eating</u> a banana.
③ The girl was <u>wearing</u> a red coat.
④ His new job is <u>delivering</u> pizzas.
⑤ The kids are <u>making</u> a sand castle.

Words　**snowman** 눈사람 (복수형 **snowmen**)　　**fruit** 과일　　**market** 시장　　**deliver** 배달하다
sand castle 모래성

7. 빈칸에 들어갈 동사의 형태가 바르게 짝지어진 것을 고르세요.

> • The baby kept _____. (cry)
> • Dad promised _____ home early. (come)

① crying – coming ② to cry – coming

③ crying – to come ④ to cry – to come

⑤ to crying – to come

8. 빈칸에 알맞은 말이 바르게 짝지어진 것을 고르세요.

> • I avoid _____ fried food at night.
> • They wish _____ Christmas holiday together.
> • We kept _____ comic books after dinner.

① to eat – to spend – reading

② to eat – spending – reading

③ eating – to spend – to read

④ eating – spending – to read

⑤ eating – to spend – reading

[9-10] 틀린 문장을 고르세요.

9.

① She loves having a pet.

② I hope seeing you again.

③ Speaking English is difficult.

④ Tony likes swimming in the sea.

⑤ My favorite activity is hiking.

10.

① Jack started to play the piano.

② Cleaning those rooms are very hard.

③ Her hobby is traveling to other countries.

④ They will not give up calling my office.

⑤ We decided to go to another restaurant.

Words **fried** 튀긴 **holiday** 휴가, 휴일 **spend** (시간을) 보내다 **pet** 반려동물
activity 활동 **country** 나라 **office** 사무실 **restaurant** 식당

11. 우리말을 영어로 바르게 옮긴 것을 고르세요.

> 그는 운전하는 것을 멈추었다.

① He stopped to drive.

② He stopped driving.

③ He drove to stop.

④ He drove stopping.

⑤ He stopped drive.

서술형
12. 우리말과 같은 뜻이 되도록 주어진 말을 사용하여 문장을 완성하세요.

> 수민이는 기타를 연주하는 것을 끝마쳤다.
>
> (finish, play the guitar)

➔ _____

_____

서술형
13. 우리말과 같은 뜻이 되도록 주어진 말을 바르게 배열하세요.

> 영어로 말하는 것은 연습이 필요하다.
>
> (speaking in / practice / English / needs)

➔ _____

_____

서술형
14. 우리말과 같은 뜻이 되도록 틀린 부분을 찾아 바르게 고쳐 쓰세요.

> We gave up to persuade Jack.
>
> (우리는 Jack을 설득하는 것을 포기했다.)

➔ _____

_____

서술형
15. 우리말과 같은 뜻이 되도록 두 보기에서 알맞은 말을 골라 문장을 완성하세요.

> 보기 I promised   보기 drink coffee
>
> My dad quit   go to the zoo

(1) 나는 동물원에 가기로 약속했다.

➔ _____

(2) 우리 아빠는 커피 마시는 것을 그만두셨다.

➔ _____

Words   **practice** 연습하다; 연습   **persuade** 설득하다

UNIT 05

전치사 1

장소, 위치

🌭 **Vocab Check!** 이번 과에서 배울 단어의 뜻을 확인하고, 모르는 단어에 체크 표시하세요.

✓ 1	sofa	몡 소파	11	spill	통 쏟다	21	fence	몡 울타리
2	gym	몡 체육관	12	carpet	몡 카펫	22	post office	몡 우체국
3	fountain	몡 분수	13	traffic light	몡 신호등	23	lake	몡 호수
4	closet	몡 벽장	14	City Hall	몡 시청	24	distance	몡 거리
5	pocket	몡 주머니	15	hide	통 숨다	25	church	몡 교회
6	grill	몡 그릴, 석쇠	16	police officer	몡 경찰관	26	roof	몡 지붕
7	plate	몡 접시	17	blow	통 (바람이) 불다	27	cage	몡 새장
8	lie	통 눕다	18	east	몡 동쪽	28	meeting	몡 회의, 모임
9	corner	몡 모서리, 모퉁이	19	west	몡 서쪽	29	mirror	몡 거울
10	barbecue	몡 바비큐	20	flow	통 흐르다	30	parking lot	몡 주차장

UNIT 05 전치사 1 (장소, 위치)

There is a drone in front of **Joe.**
Joe의 앞에 드론 한 대가 있어요.

He is going to fly it from **home** to **school.**
그는 집에서 학교까지 그것을 날릴 거예요.

His friends are at **school to see his drone.**
그의 친구들이 그의 드론을 보려고 학교에 있어요.

A 전치사 〈참고 4권 부록〉

전치사 뒤에 명사나 대명사를 써서 장소, 시간, 수단 등을 나타낼 수 있어요.

전치사	+	(대)명사

for you (당신을 위해)   **with** us (우리와 함께)
about it (그것에 관해)   **in** the shop (가게 안에서)
at the airport (공항에서)   **on** the street (거리에서)

전치사 다음에 대명사가 올 때는 반드시 목적격을 써야 해요.
with we (X) with us (O)

B 장소나 위치를 나타내는 전치사

장소나 위치를 나타낼 때 다음 전치사를 사용해요.

1. 장소의 in, at

in과 at은 장소를 나타내는 말 앞에 쓰여요. 도시, 국가와 같은 큰 장소 앞에는 주로 in을 쓰고, 상대적으로 좁은 장소 앞에는 주로 at을 써요.

in+장소, 공간 (~안에)	in Seoul (서울에) in a box (상자 안에)
at+한 지점 (~에서)	at a bus stop (버스 정류장에서) at the airport (공항에서)

We stayed **at** a hotel **in** London.

He is **at** an airport **in** Canada.

I sat **at** the table **in** the restaurant.

They are standing **at** the counter **in** the shop.

2. 위치의 on, under, in front of, behind, next to

on (~ 위에)	**on** the table (탁자 위에) **on** the paper (종이 위에)
under (~ 아래에)	**under** the chair (의자 아래에) **under** the tree (나무 아래에)
in front of (~ 앞에)	**in front of** the door (문 앞에) **in front of** me (내 앞에)
behind (~ 뒤에)	**behind** the building (건물 뒤에) **behind** the wall (벽 뒤에)
next to (~ 옆에)	**next to** the window (창문 옆에) **next to** him (그의 옆에)

> on은 표면 위에 닿아 있을 때 써요. 표면에 닿지 않고 위에 떨어져 있을 때는 over를 써요.

There are two books **on** the desk.   My cat is **under** the chair.

She was sitting **in front of** me.   A boy is hiding **behind** the tree.

Kevin put the table **next to** the window.

3. between A and B, from A to B

다음 전치사구는 A와 B에 각각 기준이 되는 사물이나 장소를 넣어 쓸 수 있어요.

between A and B (A와 B 사이에)	**between** the hospital **and** the bank (병원과 은행 사이에) **between** the desk **and** the chair (책상과 의자 사이에)
from A to B (A부터 B까지)	**from** north **to** south (북쪽부터 남쪽까지) **from** here **to** the train station (이곳부터 기차역까지)

I sat **between** Tony **and** Mike.   It's 1 km **from** here **to** the museum.

🐾 My Grammar Notes

1 _____는 명사나 대명사 앞에서 장소·시간 등을 나타낼 때 사용하는 말이다.

2 전치사 뒤에 대명사가 올 때는 _____을 쓴다.

    for he (X) → for _____ (O) (그를 위해)

3 _____ +도시, 국가, 공간 (~ 안에) / _____ +장소의 한 지점 (~에서)

    He is _____ a restaurant _____ Paris. (그는 파리에 있는 식당에 있다.)

A 전치사구와 우리말 뜻을 올바르게 연결하세요. ▸ 장소·위치의 전치사

Words

sofa 소파
Spanish 스페인의
Mexico 멕시코
fountain 분수
building 건물
street 거리

1. on the bed •   • ⓐ 침대 앞에

2. under the bed •   • ⓑ 침대 뒤에

3. behind the bed •   • ⓒ 침대 아래에

4. in front of the bed •   • ⓓ 침대 위에

5. next to the bed •   • ⓔ 침대 옆에

B 전치사가 들어갈 위치에 V 표시하세요. ▸ 장소·위치의 전치사

1. | behind | The cat is ✓ the sofa.

2. | at | I want to stay home today.

3. | in | People speak Spanish Mexico.

4. | in front of | We met the fountain.

5. | under | There is a young girl the tree.

6. | on | It's the oldest building this street.

7. | between | My sister is standing Mike and me.

8. | next to | Who's the tall guy you?

9. | from | He's going to travel Paris to London.

C 그림을 보고 ( ) 안에서 알맞은 전치사를 고르세요. 장소·위치의 전치사

Words

barbecue 바비큐
meat 고기
grill 그릴, 석쇠
plate 접시
glass 유리잔
(복수형
glasses)
fence 울타리

1. My family is having a barbecue party ((in) / on) the garden.

2. My sister and I are sitting (from / between) our parents.

3. A dog is sitting (behind / next to) my dad.

4. There is some meat (on / in) the grill.

5. Some food is (on / at) the plates.

6. Some drinks are (on / in) glasses.

7. My mom is sitting (in front of / next to) me.

8. My mom is putting her hand (on / at) the table.

9. There is a fence (in front of / behind) us.

10. Some trees stand (in front of / behind) the fence.

11. There is a barbecue grill (under / between) the table and the tree.

Practice

A ( ) 안에서 알맞은 말을 고르시오.

Words

spill 쏟다
carpet 카펫
key 열쇠
work 직장
hide 숨다
bottle 병
pocket 주머니
bus stop
버스 정류장
go
snorkeling
스노클링 하러
가다
Sydney
(호주) 시드니

1. I met Minho (at / (on) / from) the street.

2. My sister spilled milk (under / on / in) the carpet.

3. There is a car key (in / behind / for) my bag.

4. How long does it take (from / to / in) Seoul to Busan?

5. Many people drive a car from home (and / to / with) work.

6. Tom likes to read (next to / on / between) the window.

7. Who's hiding (in front of / in / behind) the door?

8. The park is (on / from / between) the school and the library.

B 보기에서 알맞은 말을 골라 **in** 또는 **at**을 사용하여 문장을 완성하세요.

| 보기 | the bottle | the sea | my pocket |
| | New York | a hotel | the bus stop |

1. I put the phone ___in my pocket___ .

2. They met Minho _____ .

3. Sam likes to go snorkeling _____ .

4. There isn't any milk _____ .

5. There are many tall buildings _____ .

6. I'll stay _____ in Sydney.

C 우리말과 같은 뜻이 되도록 알맞은 전치사를 고르세요.

Words

wastebasket
쓰레기통
police officer
경찰
bank 은행
lie 눕다
blow
(바람이) 불다
(과거형 **blew**)
east 동쪽
west 서쪽
corner
모서리, 모퉁이
airport 공항
parking lot
주차장

1. 상자 속에 사과가 있다.

→ There is an apple ((in)/ at) the box.

2. 우리는 벤치 위에 앉았다.

→ We sat (in / on) the bench.

3. 책상 아래에 쓰레기통이 있다.

→ There is a wastebasket (under / on) the desk.

4. 경찰이 은행 앞에 서 있다.

→ A police officer is standing (in front of / behind) the bank.

5. 고양이가 테이블 옆에 누워 있다.

→ The cat is lying (next to / under) the table.

6. 바람이 동쪽에서 서쪽으로 불었다.

→ The wind blew (between / from) east to west.

7. 그 가게는 병원과 극장 사이에 있다.

→ The shop is (between / behind) the hospital and the theater.

8. Denis는 길모퉁이에서 기다리고 있다.

→ Denis is waiting (in / at) the corner of the street.

9. 여기서 공항까지는 한 시간이 걸린다.

→ It takes an hour to get (at / from) here to the airport.

10. 주차장은 건물 뒤에 있다.

→ The parking lot is (behind / next to) the building.

D 우리말과 같은 뜻이 되도록 알맞은 전치사를 쓰세요.

Words

jacket 재킷
wallet 지갑
bookstore
서점
post office
우체국
station 역

1. 내 재킷은 침대 위에 있다.

→ My jacket is **on** the bed.

2. 그들은 한국에 살지 않는다.

→ They don't live _____ Korea.

3. 엄마는 지금 은행에 계신다.

→ Mom is _____ the bank now.

4. Jerry는 테이블 아래에 숨어 있었다.

→ Jerry was hiding _____ the table.

5. Kate는 Tony와 내 사이에 앉았다.

→ Kate sat _____ Tony _____ me.

6. 우리 학교 뒤에는 공원이 있다.

→ There is a park _____ our school.

7. 내 지갑에는 돈이 전혀 없다.

→ I don't have any money _____ my wallet.

8. 서점은 우체국 옆에 있다.

→ The bookstore is _____ the post office.

9. 학교 앞에 역이 있다.

→ There's a station _____ the school.

10. 그 버스는 서울에서 부산까지 간다.

→ The bus goes _____ Seoul _____ Busan.

E 밑줄 친 부분을 바르게 고쳐 쓰세요.

1. He stayed <u>at</u> Spain last month. → `in`
2. There is a clock <u>at</u> the wall. →
3. Fred was running in front of <u>I</u>. →
4. The bus stopped <u>on</u> the traffic light. →
5. I met Josh <u>in</u> the door. →
6. There are many famous museums <u>on</u> London. →
7. Mr. Park is making a speech <u>in front</u> people. →

Words

Spain 스페인
clock 시계
wall 벽
traffic light 신호등
famous 유명한
make a speech 연설하다
bakery 빵집, 제과점
lake 호수
glass door 유리문

F 우리말과 같은 뜻이 되도록 주어진 말을 바르게 배열하세요.

1. 은행은 제과점 옆에 있다. (the bakery / next / to)
   → The bank is `next to the bakery` .

2. 우리 집 뒤에는 호수가 있다. (a lake / my house / behind)
   → There is .

3. 네 앞에 유리문이 있다. (a glass door / in / of / front / you)
   → There is .

4. 나는 집에서 서울 타워까지 걸어갔다.
   (from / Seoul Tower / home / to)
   → I walked .

5. 나는 책상 밑에서 동전 몇 개를 찾았다. (desk / under / my)
   → I found a few coins .

A 우리말과 같은 뜻이 되도록 알맞은 전치사를 넣어 문장을 만드세요.

1. Emily is sleeping + the sofa.

(Emily는 소파 위에서 자고 있다.)

→ _____Emily is sleeping on the sofa._____

2. I saw many stars + the sky.

(나는 하늘에 있는 많은 별을 보았다.)

→ _____

3. There are some toys + the closet.

(벽장 아래에 몇몇 장난감이 있다.)

→ _____

4. Who is the girl + you in the picture?

(사진 속 네 뒤에 있는 소녀는 누구니?)

→ _____

B 우리말과 같은 뜻이 되도록 주어진 말을 이용하여 문장을 완성하세요.

1. 1) 나무 아래에 토끼 한 마리가 있다. (the tree)

→ There is a rabbit _____under the tree_____ .

2) 바다 밑에는 많은 물고기가 있다. (many fish, the sea)

→ _____There are many fish under the sea._____

2. 1) James는 우리 앞에 서 있다.

→ James is standing _____ .

2) 그는 많은 사람들 앞에서 노래하고 있다. (sing, many people)

→ _____

3. 1) 지구에서 달 사이의 거리는 얼마인가요? (the earth, the moon)

→ What is the distance _____?

2) 서울에서 도쿄 사이의 거리는 얼마인가요? (Seoul, Tokyo)

→ _____

4. 1) John은 우리 집 옆에 산다. (my house)

→ John lives _____.

2) 그 서점은 우리 학교 옆에 있다. (the bookstore, my school)

→ _____

C 그림과 일치하도록 주어진 단어를 이용하여 문장을 완성하세요.

1. The church is _____ **behind the red car** _____. (the red car)

2. A big tree is _____. (the church)

3. An ambulance is _____. (the hospital)

4. The post office is _____.
(the hospital, the church)

Words   **closet** 벽장   **rabbit** 토끼   **distance** 거리   **church** 교회   **ambulance** 구급차
hospital 병원

Wrap-Up Test

1. 전치사와 그 의미가 바르게 연결되지 <u>않은</u> 것을 고르세요.

① on: ~ 위에　　② under: ~ 아래에

③ next to: ~ 옆에　　④ behind: ~ 뒤에

⑤ in front of: ~ 안에

[2-4] 빈칸에 공통으로 알맞은 것을 고르세요.

2.

- Did you sing _____ the party?
- Jinsu is waiting for you _____ the door.

① in　　　② at　　　③ on

④ under　　⑤ between

3.

- There is a cat _____ the roof.
- He put his coat _____ the bed.

① in　　　② at　　　③ on

④ between　⑤ with

4.

- Three birds are _____ the cage.
- There are four seasons _____ Korea.

① in　　　② at　　　③ on

④ from　　⑤ about

5. 빈칸에 들어갈 수 <u>없는</u> 것을 고르세요.

I don't want to sit next to _____.

① him　　　　② they

③ the man　　④ the door

⑤ the tree

[6-7] 우리말과 같은 뜻이 되도록 빈칸에 알맞은 말을 쓰세요.

6.

The library is _____ our school _____ the gym.
(도서관은 우리 학교와 체육관 사이에 있다.)

7.

It is far _____ here _____
the airport.
(여기서 공항까지는 멀다.)

8. 빈칸에 알맞은 말이 바르게 짝지어진 것을 고르세요.

- The bag was next _____ the sofa.
- I walked from the hospital _____ the hair shop.
- Mary was sitting between Harry _____ Ron.

① of – to – or
② to – on – or
③ to – to – and
④ of – at – and
⑤ to – on – and

9. 우리말을 영어로 바르게 옮긴 것을 고르세요.

나는 종종 거울 앞에서 춤을 춘다.

① I often dance after the mirror.
② I often dance under the mirror.
③ I often dance behind the mirror.
④ I often dance next to the mirror.
⑤ I often dance in front of the mirror.

10. 빈칸에 들어갈 말이 나머지와 다른 것을 고르세요.

① The river flows _____ the bridge.
② There is a printer _____ the table.
③ They are relaxing _____ the tree.
④ I met Mr. Smith _____ the meeting.
⑤ Girls are sitting _____ a beach umbrella.

11. 밑줄 친 부분이 어색한 것을 고르세요.

① Is my cell phone on the table?
② The office is next City Hall.
③ The boys are in the swimming pool.
④ He is standing in front of many students.
⑤ It takes 10 minutes from the bus stop to the subway station.

Words **hair shop** 미용실 **mirror** 거울 **flow** 흐르다 **printer** 인쇄기, 프린터 **relax** 휴식을 취하다 **meeting** 회의, 모임 **City Hall** 시청 **swimming pool** 수영장

12. 틀린 문장을 고르세요.

① I lived in Canada 10 years ago.

② My best friend was behind her.

③ Kids are playing in the living room.

④ The cat is hiding behind the curtain.

⑤ I heard an interesting story about he.

13. 다음 글을 읽고, 글의 내용과 일치하지 않는 것을 고르세요.

A toy car is on the box. The box is in front of a bookshelf. The bookshelf is between the chair and a Christmas tree. A big window is behind the Christmas tree.

① The box is under a toy car.

② The bookshelf is behind the box.

③ The chair is next to the bookshelf.

④ The tree is in front of the window.

⑤ The tree is between the bookshelf and the chair.

서술형

14. 우리말과 같은 뜻이 되도록 주어진 말을 바르게 배열하세요.

그는 서점 앞에 서 있다.

(bookstore / front / he / in / is / of / the / standing)

→ _____

_____

서술형

15. 우리말과 같은 뜻이 되도록 주어진 말을 사용하여 문장을 완성하세요.

제과점은 은행 뒤에 있다.

(the bakery, the bank)

→ _____

_____

Words   **living room** 거실   **curtain** 커튼   **bookshelf** 책장

UNIT 06

전치사 2

시간, 기타

🥒 **Vocab Check!** 이번 과에서 배울 단어의 뜻을 확인하고, 모르는 단어에 체크 표시하세요.

☑ **1** plan	몡 계획	☐ **11** rope	몡 밧줄	☐ **21** noodle	몡 국수
☐ **2** ride	통 타다	☐ **12** international	혱 국제적인	☐ **22** wizard	몡 마법사
☐ **3** theater	몡 극장	☐ **13** competition	몡 경쟁; 대회	☐ **23** list	몡 목록
☐ **4** vacation	몡 방학, 휴가	☐ **14** hobby	몡 취미	☐ **24** draw	통 그리다
☐ **5** future	몡 미래	☐ **15** midnight	몡 자정	☐ **25** crayon	몡 크레용
☐ **6** cut	통 자르다	☐ **16** national	혱 나라의, 국가의	☐ **26** again	뷔 다시
☐ **7** news	몡 소식	☐ **17** turn off	(전원을) 끄다	☐ **27** Canadian	혱 캐나다의
☐ **8** be born	태어나다	☐ **18** spaceship	몡 우주선	☐ **28** present	몡 선물
☐ **9** text message	문자 메시지	☐ **19** Mars	몡 화성	☐ **29** cousin	몡 사촌
☐ **10** practice	통 연습하다	☐ **20** scarf	몡 스카프	☐ **30** farewell party	송별회

UNIT 06 전치사 2 (시간, 기타)

People are playing on a beach in the morning.
사람들은 아침에 해변에서 놀고 있어요.

A storm is coming at noon.
폭풍이 정오에 올 거예요.

They must leave the beach before noon!
그들은 정오 전에 해변을 떠나야 해요!

 시간을 나타내는 전치사
나타내는 시간의 종류의 따라 다양한 전치사를 사용해요.

1. in, at, on

in+오전[오후] / 연도 / 월 / 계절	at + 시각 / 특정 시점	on + 날짜 / 요일 / 특정한 날
in the morning (아침에) **in** 2018 (2018년에) **in** April (4월에) **in** spring (봄에)	**at** 9 o'clock (9시 정각에) **at** 6:30 (6시 30분에) **at** night (밤에) **at** lunchtime (점심시간에)	**on** May 24 (5월 24일에) **on** Sunday (일요일에) **on** Monday morning (월요일 아침에) **on** New Year's Day (설날에)

I was born **in** 2008.   Class begins **at** 9.   Winter vacation starts **on** December 21.

2. before, after, for

before (~ 전에)	**before** 8:30 (8시 30분 전에) **before** breakfast (아침 식사 전에)
after (~ 후에)	**after** work (퇴근 후에) **after** dinner (저녁 식사 후에)
for (~ 동안)	**for** a week (일주일 동안) **for** three days (3일 동안)

You must come home **before** 8 o'clock.

We often play baseball **after** school.

They stayed in Paris **for** a week.

B 그 밖의 전치사

전치사는 문맥에 따라 다양한 의미로 쓰일 수 있어요.

about (~에 관해, 대략)	about love (사랑에 관해)	about an hour (약 한 시간)
by (~을 타고)	by bus (버스를 타고)	by subway (지하철을 타고)
for (~을 위해)	for you (당신을 위해)	for the victory (승리를 위해)
to (~로, ~에게)	to the left (왼쪽으로) to me (나에게)	to school (학교로) to Jane (Jane에게)
with (~와 함께, ~을 가지고)	with him (그와 함께) with a fork (포크를 가지고)	with my friends (내 친구들과 함께) with a pencil (연필을 가지고)

The TV program is **about** animals.　　　I go to school **by** bus.

I made a special cake **for** you.　　　We went **to** the zoo yesterday.

I live **with** my grandparents.

🫘 Mini Grammar

between A and B(A와 B 사이에)와 from A to B(A부터 B까지)는 시간을 나타낼 때도 쓸 수 있어요.
You can call me **between 8 and 10 p.m.** (당신은 나에게 오후 8시와 10시 사이에 전화할 수 있어요.)
My dad works **from Monday to Friday**. (우리 아빠는 월요일부터 금요일까지 일하세요.)

🫘 My Grammar Notes

1 시간을 나타내는 전치사에는 in, at, on, before, after, for 등이 있다.

_____ the morning　　　_____ 2 p.m.　　　_____ Sunday

2 그 외에도 about (~에 관해), _____ (~을 타고), _____ (~을 위해), _____ (~로, ~에게),

_____ (~와 함께, ~을 가지고) 등의 전치사가 있다.

3 in, at, on, between A and B, from A to B는 장소와 시간의 의미 둘 다 가진다.

장소: _____ the table (탁자 위에)　　　시간: _____ Monday (월요일에)

4 전치사는 문맥에 따라 여러 가지 의미로 쓰일 수 있다.

go _____ school (~로)　　　_____ my friend (~에게)

A 보기에서 알맞은 전치사를 골라 빈칸에 쓰세요. 시간의 전치사

Words

lunchtime 점심시간
New Year's Day 설날
plan 계획
list 목록
take a shower 샤워하다

보기   in   at   on

1. [in] April
2. _____ June 5
3. _____ 2 o'clock
4. _____ 2010
5. _____ Friday
6. _____ December
7. _____ the evening
8. _____ night
9. _____ summer
10. _____ 10:20 a.m.
11. _____ Christmas Day
12. _____ lunchtime
13. _____ Saturday morning
14. _____ New Year's Day

B Jimmy의 계획표를 보고 알맞은 전치사를 고르세요. 시간의 전치사

Jimmy's Saturday Plans

have breakfast → ride a bike → make a shopping list →
have lunch → go shopping → take a shower → have dinner →
watch TV → go to bed

1. Jimmy will ride his bike (before / (after)) breakfast.

2. Jimmy will make a list (before / after) going shopping.

3. Jimmy will go shopping (before / after) lunch.

4. Jimmy will take a shower (before / after) dinner.

5. Jimmy will watch TV (before / after) dinner.

C 우리말과 같은 뜻이 되도록 ( ) 안에서 알맞은 전치사를 고르세요.

그 밖의 전치사

Words

theater 극장
weekend 주말
chopsticks
젓가락
save 모으다
cut 자르다
(과거형 cut)
knife 칼
history 역사

1. Patrick은 삼촌과 함께 산다.

→ Patrick lives (by / (with)) his uncle.

2. Alice는 우리에게 그녀의 계획에 대해 말했다.

→ Alice told us (about / to) her plans.

3. 우리는 주말마다 극장에 간다.

→ We go (for / to) the theater every weekend.

4. 한국 사람들은 젓가락으로 음식을 먹는다.

→ Korean people eat food (by / with) chopsticks.

5. 우리 아빠는 오전 9시부터 오후 7시까지 일한다.

→ My dad works (for / from) 9 a.m. to 7 p.m.

6. 나는 새 휴대전화를 사기 위해 돈을 모으고 있다.

→ I'm saving money (for / with) a new cell phone.

D 문장이 완성되도록 바르게 연결하세요.   그 밖의 전치사

1. She cut the cake   •   • ⓐ by bus.

2. I have many books   •   • ⓑ with a knife.

3. Jane went home   •   • ⓒ to the airport?

4. I bought fresh milk •   • ⓓ about history.

5. Why did you go   •   • ⓔ with the kids?

6. What did you play   •   • ⓕ for the baby.

Practice

A 주어진 말과 **in, at, on** 중 알맞은 것을 이용하여 문장을 완성하세요.

Words

Mozart
모차르트
be born
태어나다
lesson 수업
go for a walk
산책하다
farewell party 송별회
hour 시간

1. I go to sleep   at 10:30   . (10:30)

2. Mozart was born _____ . (1756)

3. I have piano lessons _____ . (Tuesdays)

4. I get up early _____ . (the morning)

5. Kevin will have a party _____ . (his birthday)

6. They sometimes go for a walk _____ . (night)

7. _____ we had a farewell party for Dan. (June 14)

B Max의 하루 일과를 보고 빈칸에 알맞은 전치사를 쓰세요.

7:00 a.m.	get up	6:00 p.m.	do homework
7:30 a.m.	have breakfast	7:00 p.m.	have dinner
8:00 a.m.	go to school	9:00 p.m.	read a book
5:00 p.m.	come home	10:00 p.m.	go to bed

1. Max gets up at 7   in   the morning.

2. He goes to school _____ breakfast.

3. He comes home _____ 5 p.m.

4. He does his homework _____ dinner.

5. He reads a book _____ an hour.

6. He goes to bed _____ reading.

C 빈칸에 공통으로 알맞은 전치사를 쓰세요.

1. Bears sleep   in   winter.

   I was born   in   September.

2. We ate lunch   noon.

   School starts   8:30 a.m.

3. I saw Tiffany   Monday.

   My birthday is   February 2nd.

4. I go to school   subway.

   Can I get there   bus?

5. Jane is talking   her boyfriend.

   I have to think   my future.

6. I went to the concert   Laura.

   Amy drew a picture   crayons.

7. I made dinner   my family.

   We stayed in Bangkok   three days.

8. Lunch break is   noon to 2 p.m.

   The bank is open   Monday to Friday.

9. She told a funny story   me.

   Jenny went   the bookstore yesterday.

10. I will arrive there   6 and 7 p.m.

    There is a park   the museum and City Hall.

D 우리말과 같은 뜻이 되도록 빈칸에 알맞은 전치사를 쓰세요.

Words

news 소식
travel 여행하다
Europe 유럽
take a photo
사진을 찍다
again 다시

1. 나는 친구들과 함께 영화를 보러 갔다.

→ I went to the movies **with** my friends.

2. Kevin에 대한 소식 들었니?

→ Did you hear the news _____ Kevin?

3. 너는 지금 슈퍼마켓에 가고 있니?

→ Are you going to go _____ the supermarket now?

4. 우리는 기차로 유럽을 여행했다.

→ We traveled around Europe _____ train.

5. 유진이는 스마트폰으로 사진을 찍었다.

→ Yujin took a photo _____ her smartphone.

6. 우리 오빠는 2주 동안 입원했다.

→ My brother was in the hospital _____ two weeks.

7. Tom은 10시에 잠자리에 든다.

→ Tom goes to bed _____ 10 o'clock.

8. 너는 8시 전에 돌아와야 한다.

→ You must come back _____ 8 o'clock.

9. 아버지가 나를 위해 새 컴퓨터를 사주셨다.

→ My dad bought a new computer _____ me.

10. Jenny와 나는 이틀 후에 다시 만났다.

→ Jenny and I met again _____ two days.

E 밑줄 친 부분을 바르게 고쳐 쓰세요.

Words

class 수업
usually
대개, 보통
vacation
방학, 휴가
hobby 취미
practice
연습하다
text message
문자 메시지

1. We have no class <u>in</u> Sunday.　→　**on**

2. What do you usually do <u>on</u> the afternoon?　→

3. We don't go to school <u>at</u> Children's Day.　→

4. My family will go <u>for</u> Canada on vacation.　→

5. Are you going to go <u>with</u> subway?　→

6. I write in my diary <u>on</u> night.　→

F 우리말과 같은 뜻이 되도록 주어진 말을 바르게 배열하세요.

1. 나는 아빠와 낚시하는 것을 좋아한다.

   (go fishing / dad / my / like / I / with / to)

   →　**I like to go fishing with my dad.**

2. Paul은 자신의 취미에 대해 이야기했다.

   (his / about / hobby / talked / Paul)

   →

3. 나는 오후 5시부터 6시까지 드럼을 연습한다.

   (I / from / 6 p.m. / the drums / practice / 5 / to)

   →

4. Andy는 반 친구들에게 문자 메시지를 보냈다.

   (sent / to / Andy / classmates / a text message / his)

   →

A 우리말과 같은 뜻이 되도록 어울리는 것끼리 선으로 연결하고, 알맞은 전치사를 넣어
문장을 만드세요.

1. I will have a party   •   • ⓐ warm milk

2. Jake went to Paris   •   • ⓑ his friend

3. Adam sent an e-mail •   • ⓒ airplane

4. Jessica eats bread   •   • ⓓ my birthday

1. 나는 내 생일에 파티를 할 것이다.

   ➔   I will have a party on my birthday.

2. Jake는 비행기를 타고 파리에 갔다.

   ➔

3. Adam은 그의 친구에게 이메일을 보냈다.

   ➔

4. Jessica는 따뜻한 우유와 함께 빵을 먹는다.

   ➔

B 우리말과 같은 뜻이 되도록 주어진 말을 이용하여 문장을 완성하세요.

1. 1) Kevin은 한 달간 병원에 있었다.

   ➔ Kevin was ____in____ the hospital ____for____ a month.

   2) 그는 일본에 3주간 머물렀다. (stay in Japan, three weeks)

      ➔ _____He stayed in Japan for three weeks._____

2. 1) 나는 아침 7시에 일어난다.

➔ I get up _____ 7 _____ the morning.

2) 나는 저녁 8시에 TV를 본다. (watch TV, evening)

➔ _____

3. 1) 나는 엄마를 위해 저녁 식사 후에 설거지를 했다.

➔ I washed the dishes _____ Mom _____ dinner.

2) 나는 Tom을 위해 방과 후에 이 책을 샀다. (buy this book, school)

➔ _____

4. 1) 나는 칼로 밧줄을 잘랐다.

➔ I cut the rope _____ a knife.

2) Kate는 새 펜으로 편지를 썼다. (write a letter, a new pen)

➔ _____

C 다음 글을 읽고, 빈칸에 알맞은 전치사를 쓰세요.

Today, there is an international baseball game. The game is ___between___ the U.S. team and the Canadian team. It will begin _____ 6 p.m. _____ October 11. This is one of the biggest competitions _____ 2019. I'm going to watch the game _____ my friends at this stadium. My friends and I are saving money _____ the game tickets.

Words   **rope** 밧줄   **international** 국제적인   **Canadian** 캐나다의   **competition** 경쟁; 대회
stadium 경기장

Wrap-Up Test

1. 밑줄 친 부분이 틀린 것을 고르세요.

① <u>in</u> January   ② <u>on</u> April 21

③ <u>at</u> midnight   ④ <u>in</u> Saturday

⑤ <u>at</u> 10:48 p.m.

[2-3] 빈칸에 공통으로 알맞은 것을 고르세요.

2.

> • The library opens _____ 9 o'clock.
>
> • Mike stayed _____ home last weekend.

① in   ② at   ③ on

④ by   ⑤ for

3.

> • The cat is lying _____ the carpet.
>
> • I was very happy _____ my birthday.

① in   ② at   ③ on

④ for   ⑤ with

4. 우리말과 같은 뜻이 되도록 빈칸에 알맞은 말이 바르게 짝지어진 것을 고르세요.

> Jake will go _____ Paris _____ plane _____ Monday.
>
> (Jake는 월요일에 비행기로 파리에 갈 것이다.)

① to – with – in   ② for – by – at

③ to – by – on   ④ in – with – on

⑤ for – with – in

5. 다음 문장이 같은 의미가 되도록 빈칸에 알맞은 말을 고르세요.

> I turned off my cell phone at 7:20. The show started at 7:30.
>
> ➔ I turned off my cell phone _____ the show.

① at   ② on

③ before   ④ after

⑤ for

6. 밑줄 친 부분을 바르게 고친 것을 고르세요.

> • I usually jog <u>at</u> the early morning.
>
> • We went to the national park <u>to</u> car.

① in – by   ② by – in

③ to – at   ④ on – for

⑤ for – with

[7-8] 밑줄 친 부분의 의미가 나머지와 <u>다른</u> 것을 고르세요.

7.

① My brother cleaned my room <u>for</u> me.

② I bought some flowers <u>for</u> Jenny.

③ I will cook spaghetti <u>for</u> you.

④ You have to wait <u>for</u> two hours.

⑤ I can fix the computer <u>for</u> you.

8.

① We went <u>to</u> the concert last night.

② Jane gave three apples <u>to</u> me.

③ Let's walk from here <u>to</u> the bus stop.

④ I will go <u>to</u> the park this weekend.

⑤ They will send the spaceship <u>to</u> Mars.

9. 우리말을 영어로 바르게 옮긴 것을 고르세요.

> 우리는 한 배우에 대한 뉴스를 보았다.

① We saw the news in an actor.

② We saw the news by an actor.

③ We saw the news with an actor.

④ We saw the news after an actor.

⑤ We saw the news about an actor.

10. 밑줄 친 부분이 올바른 것을 고르세요.

① It often snows <u>at</u> winter.

② Yunho went to Busan <u>with</u> train.

③ Kevin is going to India <u>on</u> December.

④ I met my friend Chris <u>after</u> lunch.

⑤ He bought me a scarf <u>in</u> June 11.

Words   **national** 나라의, 국가의   **spaceship** 우주선   **Mars** 화성   **scarf** 스카프

[11-12] 우리말과 같은 뜻이 되도록 빈칸에 알맞은 말을 쓰세요.

11.

J.K. Rowling wrote a story _____ a boy wizard.

(J.K. Rowling은 한 소년 마법사에 관한 이야기를 썼다.)

12.

I played computer games _____ Andy _____ school.

(나는 방과 후에 Andy와 함께 컴퓨터 게임을 했다.)

서술형

13. 빈칸에 공통으로 들어갈 말을 쓰세요.

- We will have a party _____ Friday night.
- My cousin didn't give me a present _____ Children's Day.

서술형

14. 틀린 부분을 찾아 바르게 고쳐 쓰세요.

I often have a cup of coffee on night.

➔ _____

_____

서술형

15. 우리말과 같은 뜻이 되도록 주어진 말을 바르게 배열하세요.

젓가락으로 이 국수를 먹을 수 있나요?

(these / chopsticks / can / with / noodles / you / eat)

➔ _____

_____

Words　　wizard 마법사　　cousin 사촌　　present 선물　　noodle 국수

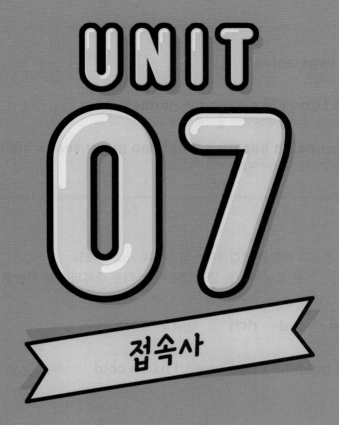

UNIT 07

접속사

🌭 **Vocab Check!** 이번 과에서 배울 단어의 뜻을 확인하고, 모르는 단어에 체크 표시하세요.

✓ **1** polar bear   몡 북극곰

2 happiness   몡 행복

3 try   통 시도하다

4 age   몡 나이

5 fail the test   시험에 낙제하다

6 headache   몡 두통

7 giraffe   몡 기린

8 enter   통 들어가다

9 thirsty   혱 목이 마른

10 trust   통 믿다, 신뢰하다

11 password   몡 비밀번호

12 log in   로그인하다

13 take off   (옷을) 벗다

14 miss   통 놓치다

15 strawberry   몡 딸기

16 lonely   혱 외로운

17 bathroom   몡 욕실, 화장실

18 desert   몡 사막

19 seed   몡 씨앗

20 dessert   몡 디저트, 후식

21 flour   몡 밀가루

22 glad   혱 기쁜

23 address   몡 주소

24 ring   통 울리다

25 graduate   통 졸업하다

26 salty   혱 짠맛이 나는

27 carry   통 옮기다

28 terrible   혱 무서운

29 rainbow   몡 무지개

30 appear   통 나타나다

접속사

> **I like fruit and vegetables.**
> 나는 과일과 채소를 좋아해요.
>
> **I like them, but I don't like eating watermelon.**
> 나는 그것들을 좋아하지만, 수박을 먹는 것은 좋아하지 않아요.
>
> **I don't like watermelon because it has too many seeds inside.**
> 수박은 안에 씨가 너무 많아서, 나는 수박을 좋아하지 않아요.

A 접속사

단어와 단어, 또는 문장과 문장을 연결해주는 말을 접속사라고 해요.
and, but, or, so는 같은 종류의 말을 연결해야 해요. 다른 종류의 말을 연결할 수 없어요.

He is ⬚ **young** ⬚ and ⬚ **rich** ⬚ . (형용사＋형용사)

⬚ **I went to the hospital** ⬚ because ⬚ **I had a cold** ⬚ . (문장＋문장)

B and, but, or, so

and, but, or, so는 같은 종류의 말을 연결하는 말이에요.

and (그리고)	비슷한 내용을 연결할 때 사용하며, '그리고', '~와'로 해석해요. 세 개 이상의 단어를 연결할 때는 마지막 단어 앞에만 and를 쓰고 나머지는 콤마(,)로 구분해요.
but (그러나)	서로 반대되는 내용을 연결할 때 사용하며, '그러나', '~이지만'으로 해석해요.
or (또는)	선택해야 하는 내용을 연결할 때 사용하며, '또는', '~이거나'로 해석해요.
so (그래서)	인과관계(원인과 결과)를 연결해요. '그래서', '~해서'라고 해석해요. so는 단어와 단어는 연결할 수 없고, 문장과 문장만 연결할 수 있어요.

I put eggs, cheese, **and** ham on the sandwich.

The movie was long **but** interesting.

Did you go out **or** stay at home last night?

It was very hot, **so** I opened the window.
　　원인　　　　　　　　　결과

when, before, after, because

when, before, after, because는 문장과 문장을 연결하는 말이에요.

when (~할 때)	**When** I was sick, I went to bed early. It was 10 a.m. **when** I got up this morning.
before (~하기 전에)	**Before** Mom comes home, I have to finish my homework. We have 10 minutes **before** the movie starts.
after (~한 후에)	**After** I do my homework, I'll go out. Can I borrow the book **after** you read it?
because (~이기 때문에)	**Because** it rained a lot, he didn't wash his car. I didn't call you **because** I lost my cell phone.

🌭 Mini Grammar

1. 의문사 when *vs.* 접속사 when `참고 2권 Unit 08`

When did you call me? (당신은 언제 내게 전화했나요?)

When you called me, I wasn't at home. (당신이 내게 전화했을 때, 나는 집에 없었어요.)

2. 전치사 before, after *vs.* 접속사 before, after `참고 Unit 06`

before와 after가 전치사로 쓰일 때는 뒤에 (대)명사가 오고, 접속사로 쓰이면 뒤에 '주어+동사'가 와요.

I'll watch TV **after** <u>dinner</u>. (나는 저녁 식사 후에 TV를 볼 거예요.)
　　　　　　　　　명사

I'll watch TV **after** <u>I</u> <u>have</u> dinner. (나는 저녁 식사를 한 후에 TV를 볼 거예요.)
　　　　　　　주어 동사

🌭 My Grammar Notes

1 _____ : 단어와 단어, 문장과 문장을 연결해 주는 말

2 and (그리고), _____ (그러나), _____ (또는), _____ (그래서)는 같은 종류의 말을 연결한다.

boys and girls (명사+_____)

He is right or wrong. (형용사+_____)

3 _____ (~할 때), _____ (~하기 전에), after (~한 후에), _____ (~이기 때문에)는 문장과 문장을 연결한다.

A 접속사를 찾아 O 표시하고, 접속사가 연결하는 말에 밑줄을 그으세요.

접속사

1. Polar bears are big and white.

2. Is it Tuesday or Wednesday?

3. She was sad, but she didn't cry.

4. Let's go out after the rain stops.

5. I make a plan before I try something.

6. My dream is to travel to Europe when I am 20.

7. It's cold outside, so I am going to wear a coat.

8. I like Sunday because I don't have to go to school.

B and, but, or, so 중 알맞은 접속사를 빈칸에 쓰세요. 접속사

1. Jane   and   I are the same age.

2. My camera is cheap,   it works well.

3. Is your sister older   younger than you?

4. He studied hard,   he failed the test.

5. I had a headache,   I went to see a doctor.

6. There are monkeys, lions   giraffes in the zoo.

7. He lies a lot,   we don't trust him.

8. Do you want to cook dinner   wash the dishes?

C ( ) 안에서 알맞은 접속사를 고르세요. < 접속사

1. Do it ((before)/ after) you forget.

2. I drank water (because / so) I was thirsty.

3. I was busy (when / because) you called me.

4. (So / Because) I forgot my password, I couldn't log in.

5. (Before / After) I finish my homework, I'll watch TV.

6. Brush your teeth (before / after) you finish eating.

7. My grandfather was handsome (when / before) he was young.

8. Please take off your shoes (before / after) you enter the room.

D 문장이 완성되도록 바르게 연결하세요. < 접속사

1. I was hungry, • • ⓐ when she reads.

2. Yunha listens to music • • ⓑ because he got up late.

3. Jack missed the bus • • ⓒ because he broke his leg.

4. Dad goes jogging • • ⓓ so I ate three bananas.

5. I turn off the computer • • ⓔ after I use it.

6. Joel can't run • • ⓕ before he has breakfast.

7. He doesn't like soccer, • • ⓖ but he likes hockey.

Practice

A 주어진 접속사가 들어갈 알맞은 위치에 V 표시하세요.

1. **and** — I like apples ✔ strawberries.

2. **but** — He is diligent, she is lazy.

3. **before** — I turn off the light I go to bed.

4. **because** — I can't help you I'm too busy.

5. **or** — Where do you live, in Seoul in Busan?

6. **so** — It is getting dark, we have to go home now.

7. **but** — These cookies look bad, they taste sweet.

Words

strawberry 딸기
diligent 부지런한
lazy 게으른
light 전등
arrive 도착하다
happiness 행복
hobby 취미 (복수형 **hobbies**)
fix 수리하다

B 빈칸에 알맞은 것을 고르세요.

1. Did he arrive late or _____ ?
   ① early ✔   ② earlier   ③ earliest

2. The man is rich, but not _____ .
   ① happy   ② happily   ③ happiness

3. Mark washed his hands and _____ sandwiches.
   ① eats   ② eating   ③ ate

4. My hobbies are playing football and _____ a bicycle.
   ① ride   ② riding   ③ to ride

5. Are you going to buy a new computer or _____ the old one?
   ① fix   ② fixed   ③ fixing

C 보기에서 알맞은 접속사를 골라 빈칸에 쓰세요.

Words

보기   and   but   or   so   because   when

1. We can go there by subway   **or**   by bus.

2. I want to stay, _____ Chris wants to leave.

3. I lost my cell phone, _____ I wasn't able to call you.

4. I got angry _____ the music was too loud.

5. Alex lived in Canada _____ he was young.

6. Amy eats a lot of candy, chocolate, _____ cookies.

leave 떠나다
lose
잃어버리다
(과거형 lost)
loud 시끄러운
young 어린
order 주문하다
desert 사막
in the
daytime 낮에
dessert
디저트, 후식
midnight 자정
fall in love
사랑에 빠지다
(과거형 fell in
love)

D 빈칸에 공통으로 알맞은 말을 쓰세요.

1. We ordered potato pizza   **and**   chicken salad.
   Jessica   **and**   I often go shopping together.

2. Deserts are hot in the daytime _____ cold at night.
   I'm not good at skating, _____ I'm good at skiing.

3. I ate some dessert _____ lunch.
   _____ my brother was born, we moved to Busan.

4. Jenny takes a shower _____ she goes to bed.
   Cinderella had to go home _____ midnight.

5. _____ is your birthday?
   Romeo and Juliet fell in love _____ they first met.

E 우리말과 같은 뜻이 되도록 빈칸에 알맞은 접속사를 쓰세요.

1. 우리 팀이 경기에서 이겼을 때, 모두가 기뻐했다.

   ➔ _When_ our team won the game, everybody was glad.

2. 그는 떠나기 전에 내 이메일 주소를 물었다.

   ➔ He asked for my e-mail address _____ he left.

3. 물이 너무 차가웠기 때문에, 우리는 수영을 하지 않았다.

   ➔ We didn't swim _____ the water was too cold.

4. 전화벨이 울릴 때, Joe는 요리를 하고 있었다.

   ➔ Joe was cooking _____ the phone rang.

5. 너는 졸업한 후에 무엇을 할 거니?

   ➔ What are you going to do _____ you graduate?

6. 나는 점심을 먹지 않았지만, 배고프지 않다.

   ➔ I didn't have lunch, _____ I'm not hungry.

7. 그 수프가 너무 짜서, 나는 먹지 않았다.

   ➔ The soup was too salty, _____ I didn't eat it.

8. 우리는 영화가 시작하기 전에 팝콘을 샀다.

   ➔ We bought some popcorn _____ the movie started.

9. 너무 무거워서 나는 저 상자를 혼자 옮길 수 없다.

   ➔ I can't carry the box alone _____ it is too heavy.

10. 비가 그친 후, 하늘에 무지개가 나타났다.

    ➔ _____ the rain stopped, a rainbow appeared in the sky.

Words

win 이기다
(과거형 won)
everybody
모든 사람
glad 기쁜
address 주소
ring 울리다
(과거형 rang)
graduate
졸업하다
salty
짠맛이 나는
carry 옮기다
alone 혼자서
heavy 무거운
rainbow
무지개
appear
나타나다

F 빈칸에 들어갈 말이 나머지와 <u>다른</u> 것을 고르세요.

1. ① We were talking   laughing.
   ② I want to help you,   I'm too busy now.
   ③ Tony studied hard,   he got a bad grade in math.

2. ① I bought some flowers   today is Mom's birthday.
   ② It's raining,   you have to bring an umbrella.
   ③ I can't call her   I don't have her phone number.

3. ① We went skiing   we were on vacation.
   ② The dog was so cute   it was a puppy.
   ③ You have to go and see a doctor   it is too late.

4. ①   Mia went on a diet, she became healthy.
   ② Please return the book   you finish it.
   ③ You should wash your hands   you eat.

G 밑줄 친 부분을 바르게 고쳐 쓰세요.

1. We can see stars <u>before</u> it gets dark. →   after

2. She took a taxi because <u>late</u>. →

3. I lost the key, <u>but</u> I can't open the locker. →

4. Eric played the guitar and <u>singing</u> a song. →

5. Pooh <u>or</u> Piglet are my favorite cartoon characters. →

6. These oranges are fresh and <u>sweetly</u>. →

A 우리말과 같은 뜻이 되도록 주어진 말을 이용하여 문장을 완성하세요.

1. 나는 피곤했기 때문에 일찍 자러 갔다. (tired)

→ I went to bed early _____ because I was tired _____.

2. 우리 형은 키가 크지만, 나는 키가 작다. (short)

→ My brother is tall, _____.

3. 날씨가 더워서 나는 아이스크림을 먹었다. (eat some ice cream)

→ It was hot, _____.

4. 너는 그 박스를 천천히, 그리고 주의 깊게 옮겨야 한다. (slowly, carefully)

→ You have to move the box _____.

5. 너는 수영하러 오전에 가니, 아니면 오후에 가니? (in the afternoon)

→ Do you go swimming in the morning _____?

B 우리말과 같은 뜻이 되도록 알맞은 접속사를 넣어 문장을 만드세요.

1. I always feel sick. + I ride a roller coaster.

(롤러코스터를 타고 나면 난 항상 멀미를 한다.)

→ _____ I always feel sick after I ride a roller coaster. _____

2. It is raining. + I watch TV at home.

(비가 올 때, 나는 집에서 TV를 본다.)

→ _____

3. I didn't wear a jacket. + It was warm.

(날씨가 따뜻했기 때문에 나는 재킷을 입지 않았다.)

→ _____

4. Can I read a comic book? + I do my homework.

(숙제하기 전에 만화책 한 권 봐도 되나요?)

→ _____

5. You must brush your teeth. + You eat chocolate.

(초콜릿을 먹고 난 후에 이를 닦아야 한다.)

→ _____

6. I was young. + I sometimes had terrible dreams.

(나는 어렸을 때, 가끔 무서운 꿈을 꾸었다.)

→ _____

C 다음 글을 읽고, 보기에서 알맞은 접속사를 골라 빈칸에 쓰세요.

보기 because   or   but   when   so

Hello, I am a singer. Many people know me now, ____**but**____ they didn't know me a few years ago. I wanted to become famous, _____ I kept singing and dancing every day. Now, I'm a big star. I'm happy _____ my dreams came true. But these days I feel sad _____ lonely. Why do I have those feelings?

 **sick** 아픈; 멀미 나는   **terrible** 무서운   **dream** 꿈   **come true** 실현되다
lonely 외로운   **feeling** 감정

Wrap-Up Test

1. 접속사와 그 의미가 <u>잘못</u> 짝지어진 것을 고르세요.

① when: ~할 때

② or: 또는

③ so: 그래서

④ after: ~하기 전에

⑤ because: ~이기 때문에

2. 단어와 단어를 연결할 수 있는 접속사가 <u>아닌</u> 것을 <u>모두</u> 고르세요. (2개)

① and   ② but   ③ or

④ when   ⑤ so

3. 두 문장이 같은 의미가 되도록 빈칸에 알맞은 것을 고르세요.

> I woke up late, so I was late for school.
> → I was late for school _____ I woke up late.

① and   ② but   ③ because

④ when   ⑤ or

[4-5] 빈칸에 알맞은 말이 바르게 짝지어진 것을 고르세요.

4.

> • The TV is old, _____ it works well.
> • The water is too hot, _____ I can't drink it.

① and – because   ② and – so

③ but – because   ④ but – so

⑤ so – because

5.

> • They gave up running and _____ rope.
> • Do you want to look in the mirror or _____ to the bathroom?
> • We wanted to borrow the book from the library, but _____.

① jump – go – wasn't there

② jump – going – it was there

③ jumping - go – being there

④ jumping – going – was there

⑤ jumping – go – it wasn't there

Words   **wake up** 일어나다   **jump rope** 줄넘기하다   **mirror** 거울   **bathroom** 욕실
borrow 빌리다

6. 빈칸에 들어갈 수 <u>없는</u> 것을 고르세요.

> I had some snacks before _____.

① dinner　　　② have lunch

③ the train arrived　④ the teacher came

⑤ the game started

7. 우리말을 영어로 바르게 옮긴 것을 고르세요.

> 나는 슬플 때 코미디를 본다.

① I watch comedies so I feel sad.

② I watch comedies when I feel sad.

③ I watch comedies, and I feel sad.

④ When I watch comedies, I feel sad.

⑤ I watch comedies before I feel sad.

8. 틀린 문장을 고르세요.

① He is tall and handsome.

② I'm happy because I passed the test.

③ Marie likes math, but I don't like it.

④ Did you go out or watching TV last night?

⑤ I am too fat, so I can't wear the skirt.

9. 밑줄 친 부분을 바르게 고친 것을 고르세요.

> • He hurt his leg, <u>or</u> he didn't go to hospital.
> • <u>Because</u> I came to Korea, I was in Spain.

① but – When　　② so – After

③ but – Before　④ but – So

⑤ so – When

10. 밑줄 친 **when**의 쓰임이 나머지와 **다른** 것을 고르세요.

① Help me <u>when</u> you have time.

② <u>When</u> I was born, my father was 30.

③ <u>When</u> I was young, I liked playing soccer.

④ <u>When</u> did you fly in an airplane for the first time?

⑤ <u>When</u> I was walking down the street, I met Jack.

Words　**snack** 간식　**comedy** 코미디, 희극　**math** 수학　**skirt** 치마　**hurt** 다치게 하다
fly 날다; 비행하다　**airplane** 비행기　**for the first time** 처음으로

11. 빈칸에 공통으로 들어갈 말을 쓰세요.

- What are you going to do _____ school?

- _____ I saw the horror movie, I had a bad dream.

12. 우리말과 같은 뜻이 되도록 주어진 말을 이용하여 문장을 완성하세요.

Peter can't go on a picnic _____

_____ _____ _____ .

(sick)

(Peter는 아파서 소풍을 가지 못한다.)

13. 우리말과 같은 뜻이 되도록 주어진 말을 바르게 배열하세요.

나는 여기에 오기 전에 점심을 먹었다.

(lunch / I / here / came / before / had / I)

→ _____

_____

14. <u>틀린</u> 부분을 찾아 바르게 고쳐 쓰세요.

I decided to speak and writing in English every day.

→ _____

_____

15. 보기에서 알맞은 말을 골라 알맞은 접속사를 이용해 문장을 완성하세요.

보기 I can't bake cookies.
      It is broken.

(1) Don't touch this bottle _____

_____ .

(2) There is no flour, _____

_____ .

Words　**horror movie** 공포 영화　**go on a picnic** 소풍 가다　**bake** (음식을) 굽다
broken 고장 난; 깨진　**touch** 만지다　**bottle** 병　**flour** 밀가루

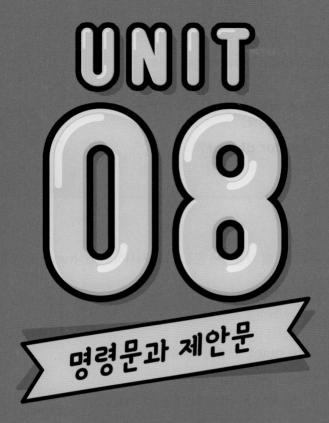

UNIT 08

명령문과 제안문

🥒 **Vocab Check!**   이번 과에서 배울 단어의 뜻을 확인하고, 모르는 단어에 체크 표시하세요.

✓ **1** smoke	통 담배를 피우다	**11** comic	형 웃긴, 코미디의	**21** afraid	형 두려워하는
2 volume	명 음량, 볼륨	**12** medicine	명 약	**22** rule	명 규칙
3 cross	통 건너다	**13** seat belt	명 안전벨트	**23** hallway	명 복도
4 toothache	명 치통	**14** enough	형 충분한	**24** fight	통 싸우다
5 truth	명 사실, 진실	**15** trash	명 쓰레기	**25** full	형 배부른
6 quiet	형 조용한	**16** pick	통 고르다; 꺾다	**26** join	통 가입하다
7 inside	부 안에	**17** rude	형 무례한	**27** painting	명 그림
8 stair	명 계단	**18** stranger	명 낯선 사람	**28** living room	명 거실
9 turn	통 돌다; 변하다	**19** stop by	~에 잠시 들르다	**29** honest	형 정직한
10 immediately	부 즉시, 바로	**20** soda	명 탄산음료	**30** ground	명 땅, 바닥

UNIT 08 명령문과 제안문

Darling! Stop playing computer games.
얘야! 컴퓨터 게임을 그만하렴.

Let's go out. It helps you refresh yourself.
나가자. 기분 전환하는 데 도움이 된단다.

Why don't we go out for dinner?
저녁 식사하러 가는 게 어떠니?

 명령문

명령문은 상대방에게 지시할 때 사용하는 문장이며, 지시하는 대상(you)이 명확하므로 주어가 없어요.

1. 명령문의 기본 형태: ~해라

명령문은 기본적으로 동사원형으로 시작해요.

동사원형 ~ (~해라)	**Be** quiet. (조용히 하세요.) **Sit** down. (앉으세요.) **Stand** up, please. (일어나 주세요.)

> 명령문의 앞이나 뒤에 please를 쓰면 더 공손한 표현이 돼요.

2. 명령문의 부정형: ~하지 마라

명령문의 부정형은 동사원형 앞에 Don't를 써서 나타내요.
Don't 대신 Never를 쓰면 더 강한 부정의 의미를 나타낼 수 있어요.

Don't[Never] +동사원형 ~ (~하지 마라)	**Don't be** rude. (무례하게 굴지 마세요.) **Don't walk** around. (돌아다니지 마세요.) **Please don't talk** now. (제발 지금 말하지 마세요.) **Never say** goodbye. (안녕이라는 말은 절대 하지 마세요.)

 Mini Grammar

제안하는 말에는 다음과 같은 답변을 할 수 있어요.
Sounds good. (좋아요.) / Okay. (좋아요.) / That's a great idea. (좋은 생각이에요.)
I'm sorry, but I can't. (죄송하지만 안 되겠어요.)

B 제안문

제안문은 상대방에게 무엇인가 제안할 때 쓰는 문장이에요.

1. Let's 제안문: ~하자

Let's 제안문은 기본적으로 동사원형 앞에 Let's를 써서 나타내고, 명령문처럼 주어가 없어요.

Let's + 동사원형 ~ (~하자)	**Let's go** swimming. (수영하러 가자.) **Let's eat** out tonight. (오늘 밤에는 외식하자.)

2. Let's 제안문의 부정형: ~하지 말자

Let's 제안문의 부정형은 Let's 뒤에 not을 붙여요.

Let's not + 동사원형 ~ (~하지 말자)	**Let's not go** to the movies. (영화를 보러 가지 말자.) **Let's not take** a taxi. (택시를 타지 말자.)

3. 기타 표현들

제안할 때 Let's 말고도 다음과 같은 다양한 표현들을 쓸 수 있어요.

Shall we + 동사원형 ~? (~할래?)	**Shall we dance?** (춤출까요?) **Shall we go** now? (이제 갈까요?)
Why don't we[you] + 동사원형 ~? (~하는 게 어때?)	**Why don't we go** to the library? (도서관에 가는 게 어떨까요?)
What[How] about + (동)명사 ~? (~는 어때?, ~하는 게 어때?)	**What about pizza** for lunch? (점심으로 피자 어때요?) **How about watching TV?** (TV를 보는 게 어떨까요?)

🌭 My Grammar Notes

1 명령문은 주어를 생략하고 바로 _____을 써서 '~해라'의 의미를 나타낸다.

2 동사 앞에 _____ 또는 Never를 붙여 '~하지 마라'의 의미를 나타낸다.

3 'Let's + 동사원형'은 제안하는 표현으로 '_____'의 의미를 나타낸다.
  '~하지 말자'라고 할 때는 Let's 뒤에 _____을 붙인다.

4 제안할 때는 'Shall we + 동사원형 ~?', '_____ don't we[you] + 동사원형 ~?',
  'What[_____] about + (동)명사 ~?' 등을 이용할 수도 있다.

A 표지판이 의미하는 말을 연결하세요. 〈 명령문

1. •
2. •
3. •
4. •
5. •

- ⓐ Don't ride a skateboard.
- ⓑ Don't use a cell phone.
- ⓒ Don't drink alcohol.
- ⓓ Don't take pictures.
- ⓔ Don't smoke here.

Words

skateboard
스케이트보드
alcohol 술
smoke
담배를 피우다
turn down
(볼륨을) 줄이다
volume
음량, 볼륨
cross 건너다
truth
사실, 진실

B ( ) 안에서 알맞은 것을 고르세요. 〈 명령문

1. (Look / Looking) at me, please.

2. (Bring / To bring) your umbrella.

3. (Turns / Turn) down the volume.

4. (Don't eat / Not eat) too much pizza.

5. (Go don't / Never go) to bed late.

6. (Don't play / Doesn't play) computer games.

7. (Never cross / Cross never) the street here.

8. (Telling / Tell) me the truth.

C ( ) 안에서 알맞은 것을 고르세요. 제안문

1. Let's ((see)/ saw) this movie.

2. Let's (make / making) some cookies.

3. Let's (play / plays) tennis together.

4. Let's (be / do) quiet in church.

5. Let's (go not / not go) shopping.

6. (Not let's / Let's not) listen to loud music.

Words

quiet 조용한
church 교회
loud (소리가)
큰, 시끄러운
fruit 과일
eat out
외식하다
pasta 파스타
accident 사고

D 우리말과 같은 뜻이 되도록 알맞은 것을 고르세요. 제안문

1. 과일을 좀 사자.

   → ((Let's) / Let's not) buy some fruit.

2. 오늘 밤에 외식할래?

   → (Will we / Shall we) eat out tonight?

3. 택시를 타는 게 어때?

   → (Why do you / Why don't you) take a taxi?

4. 10시에 만나는 게 어때?

   → (When about / How about) meeting at ten?

5. 저녁으로 파스타 어때?

   → (What about / Why about) pasta for dinner?

6. 그 사고에 대해 이야기하지 말자.

   → (Let's / Let's not) talk about the accident.

Practice

A 명령문으로 바꿀 때 빈칸에 알맞은 말을 쓰세요.

1. You have to clean your room.

→ **Clean** your room.

2. You may not eat in the library.

→ _____ in the library.

3. You don't have to worry about that.

→ _____ about that.

4. You must be quiet in class.

→ _____ quiet in class.

5. You can't sing songs here at night.

→ _____ songs here at night.

Words

worry 걱정하다
dirty 더러운
snack 간식
heavy 무거운
help 돕다
make noise
시끄럽게 하다
enough
충분한
give up
포기하다

B 빈칸에 **Let's** 또는 **Let's not** 중 알맞은 말을 쓰세요.

1. This room is so dirty. **Let's** clean it.

2. I'm hungry now. _____ have some snacks.

3. It's raining. _____ go for a walk.

4. Tomorrow is Mom's birthday. _____ have a party.

5. The old man has a heavy bag. _____ help him.

6. My sister is sleeping. _____ make too much noise.

7. I have to do my homework. _____ go to the movies.

8. We still have enough time. _____ give up.

C 두 문장의 의미가 같도록 빈칸에 알맞은 말을 쓰세요.

1. Let's go to the park.

   = <u>Why</u> <u>don't</u> we <u>go</u> to the park?

2. How about playing soccer outside?

   = _____ _____ soccer outside.

3. Let's start today's class.

   = _____ _____ start today's class?

4. Why don't we go camping this weekend?

   = _____ _____ camping this weekend.

5. Let's take a bus to the airport.

   = What _____ _____ a bus to the airport?

D 주어진 문장을 지시대로 바꿔 쓰세요.

1. You have to listen to me carefully. (명령문으로)

   → <u>Listen to me carefully.</u>

2. We are going to the movies tonight. (Let's 제안문으로)

   → _____

3. You must not be late for a meeting again. (명령문으로)

   → _____

4. Help that little child. (Why don't you ~? 제안문으로)

   → _____

5. You have to wear a seat belt when you drive. (명령문으로)

   → _____

E 우리말과 같은 뜻이 되도록 보기의 말을 이용하여 문장을 완성하세요.

보기 turn send be ride try take have swim buy

1. 네 방의 불을 꺼라.

→ ___Turn___ off the light in your room.

2. 여기서 사진을 찍을까요?

→ Shall _____ a picture here?

3. 학교에 다시는 지각하지 말아라.

→ _____ late for school again.

4. 수업 중에는 문자 메시지를 보내지 마세요.

→ _____ text messages in class.

5. 오늘은 자전거를 타지 말자.

→ _____ bikes today.

6. Jane을 위해서 초콜릿 케이크를 사자.

→ _____ a chocolate cake for Jane.

7. 같이 점심 식사할래요?

→ _____ lunch with me?

8. 우리 저 수영장에서 수영하는 게 어때?

→ _____ in that

swimming pool?

9. 중국 음식을 먹어보는 게 어때?

→ _____ Chinese food?

F 밑줄 친 부분을 바르게 고쳐 쓰세요.

Words

rude 무례한
stranger
낯선 사람
cello 첼로
climb 오르다
mountain 산
soda 탄산음료
afraid
두려워하는
watch one's step
발밑을 조심하다
stair 계단

1. <u>Are</u> a good girl. → Be

2. Let's <u>goes</u> out for lunch. →

3. <u>Be not</u> rude to strangers. →

4. <u>Turning off</u> your cell phone, please. →

5. <u>Not let's</u> play the cello. →

6. <u>Doesn't</u> touch that big dog. →

7. Why don't we <u>taking</u> a picture here? →

8. Shall we <u>sang</u> a song for her birthday? →

9. How about <u>play</u> baseball? →

10. <u>About what</u> this red skirt? →

11. Let's <u>send not</u> him a card. →

12. Katie, <u>takes</u> an umbrella with you. →

13. Let's <u>climbing</u> the mountain now. →

14. Why don't you <u>buying</u> these shoes? →

15. <u>Drink never</u> too much soda. →

16. Don't <u>being</u> afraid. →

17. How about <u>go</u> shopping? →

18. <u>Watching</u> your step on stairs. →

A 우리말과 같은 뜻이 되도록 주어진 말을 바르게 배열하세요.

1. 도서관에서는 조용히 해. (quiet / be / in the library)

→ _____ Be quiet in the library. _____

2. 늦은 밤에는 아무것도 먹지 마. (late at night / don't / eat / anything)

→ _____

3. 지금 바로 스케이트 타러 가자. (right now / let's / skating / go)

→ _____

4. 그 공포 영화는 보지 말자. (see / that horror movie / let's / not)

→ _____

5. 이 토스트를 먹어 보는 게 어때? (why / you / don't / try / this toast)

→ _____

6. 브라질로 여행을 가는 게 어때? (about / how / traveling / to Brazil)

→ _____

B 우리말과 같은 뜻이 되도록 주어진 말을 이용하여 문장을 만드세요.

1. 배낭을 탁자 위에 두어라.   put / the backpack / on the table

→ _____ Put the backpack on the table. _____

2. 디즈니랜드에 가는 게 어때?   what / go to Disneyland

→ _____

3. 이 꽃들을 꺾지 말자.   pick / these flowers

➔ _____

4. 우리 차를 좀 마실까?   shall / have / some tea

➔ _____

5. 그 문제에 대해 걱정하지 마.   worry about / that problem

➔ _____

6. 우리 함께 공부하는 게 어때?   why / study / together

➔ _____

7. 디저트로 쿠키를 먹자.   eat cookies / for dessert

➔ _____

C 다음 글을 읽고, <u>틀린</u> 부분을 찾아 표시한 다음, 고쳐서 다시 써보세요.

Classroom Rules

- Keep the classroom clean.
- Listens carefully to your teacher.
- Wash your hands before lunch.
- Not run in the hallway.
- Let's don't fight with classmates.
- Don't never use cell phones in class.

---

❶ _____ Never run in the hallway. _____

❷ _____

❸ _____

❹ _____

 **Words**   **backpack** 배낭   **pick** 고르다; 꺾다   **classroom** 교실   **rule** 규칙   **keep** 유지하다
hallway 복도   **fight** 싸우다   **classmate** 반 친구

Wrap-Up Test

1. 부정문으로 만들 때 **not**이 들어갈 위치를 고르세요.

① Let's ② join ③ the ④ baseball team ⑤ .

2. 빈칸에 알맞은 말을 고르세요.

It's too late at night. _____ play the piano now.

① Be   ② Let's   ③ Don't

④ Please   ⑤ Do

3. 두 문장이 같은 의미가 되도록 빈칸에 알맞은 것을 고르세요.

What about visiting the museum tomorrow?

= _____ about visiting the museum tomorrow?

① When   ② Why   ③ How

④ Where   ⑤ Who

4. 빈칸에 알맞은 말이 바르게 짝지어진 것을 고르세요.

- Don't _____ over there. It's dangerous.
- I like this painting. What about _____ it for our living room?

① go – buy   ② go – buying

③ going – buy   ④ going – buying

⑤ to go – buy

5. 빈칸에 들어갈 수 <u>없는</u> 것을 고르세요.

How about _____?

① playing basketball

② a comic movie for fun

③ fried chicken for dinner

④ hiking up the mountain

⑤ talk in English with your friend

Words   **join** 가입하다   **visit** 방문하다   **dangerous** 위험한   **painting** 그림   **living room** 거실   **comic** 웃긴, 코미디의   **hike** 도보 여행을 가다

6. 밑줄 친 부분을 바르게 고친 것을 고르세요.

> • Why don't you <u>helping</u> the child?
> • Please <u>are</u> careful when you cross the road.

① help – be
② to help – be
③ help – being
④ helped – to be
⑤ to help – being

7. 빈칸에 들어갈 말로 적절한 것을 고르세요.

> A: I have a toothache. I can't eat anything.
> B: _____

① Shall we eat out for dinner?
② Go to the dentist right now.
③ Let's not take some medicine.
④ Why don't you have more chocolate?
⑤ How about going to buy some candy?

8. 우리말을 영어로 바르게 옮긴 것을 고르세요.

> 친구들에게 친절해라.

① Let's kind to your friends.
② Being kind to your friends.
③ Kind to your friends, please.
④ Be kind to your friends.
⑤ Never be kind to your friends.

9. 의미하는 바가 나머지와 다른 것을 고르세요.

① Let's order pizza for lunch.
② Shall we order pizza for lunch?
③ What about ordering pizza for lunch?
④ Why didn't we order pizza for lunch?
⑤ How about ordering pizza for lunch?

10. 틀린 문장을 고르세요.

① Don't listen to loud music.
② Be honest with your friends.
③ Let's eat not fast food.
④ How about taking a break now?
⑤ Never throw any trash on the ground.

Words   **careful** 조심하는   **cross** (가로질러) 건너다   **toothache** 치통   **dentist** 치과의사
medicine 약   **order** 주문하다   **honest** 정직한   **take a break** 휴식을 취하다
throw 던지다   **trash** 쓰레기   **ground** 땅, 바닥

11. 대화가 <u>어색한</u> 것을 고르세요.

① A: Please turn on the radio.

   B: Okay, I will.

② A: Let's go swimming in the pool.

   B: Okay. Don't swim.

③ A: Shall we go to the beach?

   B: Sounds great!

④ A: How about eating some more steak?

   B: No, thanks. I'm full.

⑤ A: Don't go outside. It's too cold.

   B: Yes, I will stay inside.

서술형

12. 두 문장이 같은 의미가 되도록 빈칸에 알맞은 말을 쓰세요.

Let's go to the concert.

= _____ _____ _____

   go to the concert?

서술형

13. 우리말과 같은 뜻이 되도록 주어진 말을 바르게 배열하세요.

늦게까지 컴퓨터 게임을 하지 마라.

(late / computer games / don't / play)

➜ _____

_____

서술형

14. <u>틀린</u> 부분을 찾아 바르게 고쳐 쓰세요.

Move never immediately when the traffic light turns red.

➜ _____

_____

서술형

15. 우리말과 같은 뜻이 되도록 주어진 말을 사용하여 문장을 완성하세요.

우리 집에 잠깐 들르는 게 어때요?

(how, stop by, my place)

➜ _____

_____

 **Words**   **full** 배부른   **inside** 안에   **move** 움직이다   **immediately** 즉시, 바로   **turn** 돌다; 변하다   **stop by** ~에 잠시 들르다

UNIT 09

감탄문

부가의문문

🥒 **Vocab Check!** 이번 과에서 배울 단어의 뜻을 확인하고, 모르는 단어에 체크 표시하세요.

✓ **1**	record	몡 기록	**11**	picture	몡 그림, 사진	**21**	be in trouble	곤경에 처하다
2	brilliant	혱 훌륭한, 멋진	**12**	exciting	혱 신나는	**22**	race	몡 경주, 시합
3	horrible	혱 무시무시한	**13**	suit	몡 정장	**23**	awesome	혱 기막히게 좋은
4	surprising	혱 놀라운	**14**	hero	몡 영웅	**24**	amazing	혱 멋진, 놀라운
5	squirrel	몡 다람쥐	**15**	stupid	혱 멍청한	**25**	generous	혱 후한, 너그러운
6	wide	혱 (폭이) 넓은	**16**	perfect	혱 완벽한	**26**	recipe	몡 요리법
7	spider	몡 거미	**17**	acorn	몡 도토리	**27**	different	혱 다른
8	insect	몡 곤충	**18**	French	몡 프랑스인	**28**	colorful	혱 (색이) 다채로운
9	come along	함께 가다	**19**	information	몡 정보	**29**	bright	혱 밝은
10	strange	혱 이상한	**20**	clear	혱 (날씨가) 맑은	**30**	special	혱 특별한

UNIT 09 감탄문과 부가의문문

A: That runner runs very fast, doesn't he?
저 주자는 매우 빨리 달리네요, 그렇지 않아요?

B: Yes, he does. How fast he is!
네, 그래요. 어쩜 저리 빠를까!

A: What a wonderful player!
정말 멋진 선수예요!

 감탄문: 정말 ~하구나!

놀라움과 감탄을 표현하는 감탄문에는 how로 시작하는 감탄문과 what으로 시작하는 감탄문이 있어요.

종류	특징	어순
how 감탄문	바로 뒤에 형용사[부사]	How + 형용사[부사] (+주어+동사)!
what 감탄문	뒤에 '형용사+명사'	What(+a/an)+형용사+명사 (+주어+동사)!

He is very kind. ⇨ **How kind** (he is)!

The game is exciting. ⇨ **How exciting** (the game is)!

She is a very pretty girl. ⇨ **What a pretty girl** (she is)!

The books are interesting. ⇨ **What interesting books** (they are)!

1. 감탄문 끝에 오는 주어와 동사는 생략할 때가 많아요.
2. 명사가 복수형일 때는 앞에 a/an을 쓰지 않아요.

 부가의문문: 그렇지 (않니)?

부가의문문은 자신이 한 말에 동의를 구하거나 재확인할 때 문장 뒤에 부가적으로 붙이는 의문문이에요.

1. 부가의문문 만들기

> 긍정문은 부정형을,
> 부정문은 긍정형을
> 사용하기
>
> ⇩

You **are** bored, **aren't** you?
　　긍정문　　　　　　부정형

You **don't** know him, **do** you?
　　부정문　　　　　　긍정형

시제는 앞 문장에 맞추기	Tom **ate** pizza, **didn't** he? 　　과거　　　　　　과거 They **are** tired, **aren't** they? 　　현재　　　　　　현재

⇩

주어는 대명사로 바꾸기	**Jenny** can't swim, can **she**? **Jake and I** will meet here, won't **we**?

2. 여러 가지 부가의문문

종류	어순	
be동사의 부가의문문	be동사 (+not)+대명사?	**They aren't** sad now, **are they**?
일반동사의 부가의문문	do / did (+not)+대명사?	**Jeff plays** the piano well, **doesn't he?**
조동사의 부가의문문	조동사 (+not)+대명사?	**You can** drive, **can't you**?

🫛 **Mini Grammar**

부가의문문에 대한 대답은 질문과 상관없이 내용이 긍정이면 yes, 부정이면 no로 답해요.
You don't like tea, **do you**? (당신은 차를 좋아하지 않지요, 그렇죠?)
– **Yes**, I do. (아니요, 좋아해요.) / **No**, I don't. (네, 좋아하지 않아요.)

🫛 **My Grammar Notes**

1 감탄문: '정말 ~하구나!'라는 의미의 문장으로 _____나 _____으로 시작한다.
   (1) _____+형용사/부사 (+주어+동사)!
   (2) What(+a/an)+_____+_____ (+주어+동사)!

2 _____: 문장 뒤에 덧붙여서 '그렇지 (않니)?'라는 의미를 나타내는 의문문으로 앞에서 말한 내용을
   확인하거나 동의를 구할때 쓴다.
   (1) 긍정문 뒤에는 부정, 부정문 뒤에는 _____의 부가의문문이 온다.
   (2) 부가의문문의 _____는 앞 문장의 시제와 일치시킨다.
   (3) 부가의문문의 주어는 앞 문장의 주어를 _____로 바꿔서 쓴다.

A 감탄문이면 느낌표(!)를 쓰고, 의문문이면 물음표(?)를 쓰세요. ◀ 감탄문

1. How is the weather today   **?**

2. What a beautiful day it is

3. How pretty she is

4. How old is your sister

5. What a brilliant idea

6. What's the name of these flowers

7. What a nice picture it is

8. How much is the cup

9. How big this building is

B ( ) 안에서 알맞은 것을 고르세요. ◀ 감탄문

1. (What / How) a horrible story!

2. Look! (What / How) cute that boy is!

3. (What / How) surprising news!

4. (What / How) a difficult question!

5. (What / How) interesting!

6. (What / How) cheap the bag is!

7. (What / How) an amazing song!

C　**알맞은 것을 연결하세요.** 부가의문문

1. It is very cold, ·　　　　　　· ⓐ don't we?

2. You can't help me, ·　　　　· ⓑ can you?

3. Brian and I study hard, ·　　· ⓒ isn't it?

4. She didn't eat pizza, ·　　　· ⓓ are they?

5. Jinsu likes swimming, ·　　· ⓔ did she?

6. Spiders aren't insects, ·　　· ⓕ didn't they?

7. We didn't sleep well, ·　　· ⓖ doesn't he?

8. They did a good job, ·　　　· ⓗ did we?

Words

spider 거미
insect 곤충
have a great time 즐거운 시간을 보내다
come along 함께 가다
solve (문제를) 풀다
problem 문제
take a class 수업을 듣다

D　**( ) 안에서 알맞은 것을 고르세요.** 부가의문문

1. She is staying in Paris, (is she / isn't she)?

2. He wasn't at the party, (did he / was he)?

3. John likes skating, (does he / doesn't he)?

4. We had a great time, (don't we / didn't we)?

5. You won't come along with me, (will you / won't you)?

6. Jane can solve this problem, (can she / can't she)?

7. They didn't take this class, (do they / did they)?

8. The boys are not from Canada, (are they / are the boys)?

A 감탄문을 바르게 쓴 것을 고르세요.

1. ① What strange!   ② How strange! ✓

2. ① What a smart dog!   ② How a smart dog!

3. ① How funny is the story!   ② How funny the story is!

4. ① What beautiful a picture!   ② What a beautiful picture!

5. ① What an exciting game is!   ② What an exciting game it is!

6. ① How nice your suit is!   ② How nice your suit it is!

7. ① What a big melon is!   ② What a big melon it is!

B 주어진 말을 바르게 배열하여 감탄문을 완성하세요.

1. (lazy / a / girl / what)

   → _____ What a lazy girl! _____

2. (an / movie / what / exciting)

   → _____

3. (great / a / what / is / it / chance)

   → _____

4. (expensive / is / how / the bag)

   → _____

5. (the man / generous / is / how)

   → _____

6. (comfortable / are / how / these shoes)

   → _____

C 빈칸에 알맞은 것을 고르세요.

1. That isn't our bag, _____?
   ✓① is it   ② are they   ③ isn't it

2. She can't finish a marathon, _____?
   ① can she   ② can't she   ③ does she

3. Sumi and Jisu are twins, _____?
   ① aren't we   ② aren't you   ③ aren't they

4. Kevin will come tonight, _____?
   ① will he   ② won't he   ③ won't Kevin

5. Peter doesn't read a newspaper, _____?
   ① did he   ② does he   ③ is he

6. You didn't do your homework last night, _____?
   ① were you   ② do you   ③ did you

Words

twins 쌍둥이
newspaper 신문
last night 지난밤
win first prize 1등을 하다
Chinese 중국어
attend 참석하다
be interested in ~에 흥미[관심]가 있다
history 역사

D 부가의문문을 완성하세요.

1. The weather is nice, **isn't it** ?

2. Ann doesn't work hard, _____?

3. David won first prize, _____?

4. You can't speak Chinese, _____?

5. They'll attend the fashion show, _____?

6. You are interested in Korean history, _____?

E 우리말과 같은 뜻이 되도록 주어진 말을 이용하여 문장을 완성하세요.

Words

golf 골프
French 프랑스인
information 정보
sky 하늘
clear (날씨가) 맑은
lovely 사랑스러운

1. 너는 골프를 칠 수 있지, 그렇지 않니? (play)

→ You   can   play   golf,   can't   you   ?

2. Vincent는 프랑스인 맞지, 그렇지 않니? (be)

→ Vincent _____ French, _____ _____ ?

3. 수진이는 음악을 듣는 것을 좋아해, 그렇지 않니? (like)

→ Sujin _____ listening to music, _____ _____ ?

4. 그들은 이 책에서 정보를 조금도 얻지 않았어, 그렇지? (get)

→ They _____ _____ any information from this book,

_____ _____ ?

F 두 문장이 비슷한 의미가 되도록 빈칸에 알맞은 말을 쓰세요.

1. Look! The building is very tall.

→ Look!   How   tall   the building is!

2. He is a really strange man.

→ _____ _____ _____ man he is!

3. Wow! The sky is really clear.

→ Wow! _____ _____ the sky is!

4. She is a very lovely girl.

→ _____ _____ _____ _____ she is!

5. That tree is almost 150 years old.

→ _____ _____ that tree is!

126 - Grammar Bean 4

G 주어진 말을 이용하여 대화를 완성하세요.

Words

doll 인형
You're welcome. 천만에요.
glad 기쁜
do one's best 최선을 다하다
Have a seat. 앉으세요.
series 시리즈
awesome 기막히게 좋은, 엄청난
stupid 멍청한
arrive 도착하다

1. A: What a pretty doll! Thank you. (pretty)

   B: You're welcome. I'm glad you like it.

2. A: My sister passed the exam!

   B: She _____ her best, _____ she? (do)

3. A: Have a seat here, please.

   B: Thank you. _____ _____ you are! (kind)

4. A: You will _____ me, _____? (help)

   B: Of course I will.

5. A: Jay, did you see the movie?

   B: Yes. _____ _____ _____ story! (sad)

6. A: I'm watching the Avengers series these days.

   B: It _____ really awesome, _____ _____? (be)

H 밑줄 친 부분을 바르게 고쳐 쓰세요.

1. How <u>she fast</u> runs! → fast she

2. <u>How a stupid</u> I am! →

3. I'm not late, <u>are you</u>? →

4. <u>What lazy</u> boy he is! →

5. You will come to the party, <u>will you</u>? →

6. They arrived yesterday, <u>weren't they</u>? →

7. You can't solve the problem, <u>do you</u>? →

A 우리말과 같은 뜻이 되도록 보기의 단어를 이용하여 문장을 완성하세요.

> 보기   like   save   wide   delicious   perfect   swim

1. 그는 정말 완벽해!

→ ___How___ ___perfect___ he is!

2. 이 스파게티는 정말 맛있어!

→ _____ _____ spaghetti this is!

3. 그 도로는 정말 넓어!

→ _____ _____ the road is!

4. 너는 수영할 수 없어, 그렇지?

→ You _____ _____, _____ _____?

5. Peter는 Cindy를 좋아해, 그렇지 않니?

→ Peter _____ Cindy, _____ _____?

6. 그 영웅은 많은 사람들을 구할 수 있어, 그렇지 않니?

→ The hero _____ _____ many people, _____ _____ ?

B 우리말과 같은 뜻이 되도록 주어진 말을 이용하여 문장을 만드세요.

1. 1) 너는 피곤하지, 그렇지 않니?

→ You ___are___ tired, ___aren't___ ___you___ ?

2) 너는 일본인이지, 그렇지 않니? (Japanese)

→ ___You are Japanese, aren't you?___

2. 1) 정말 용감한 소녀구나! (brave)

➜ _____ _____ _____ girl!

2) 정말 작은 강아지구나! (small, puppy)

➜ _____

3. 1) Amy는 내 전화번호를 몰라, 그렇지? (know)

➜ Amy doesn't _____ my phone number, _____ _____?

2) Danny는 내 이름을 몰라, 그렇지? (my name)

➜ _____

4. 1) 너는 나에게 특별한 요리법을 가르쳐줄 거야, 그렇지 않니? (teach)

➜ You _____ _____ me a special recipe, _____ _____?

2) 최 선생님은 너에게 과학을 가르쳐주실 거야, 그렇지 않니? (Mr. Choi, science)

➜ _____

C **다음 글을 읽고, 밑줄 친 부분을 바르게 고쳐 쓰세요.**

Last October, I went hiking alone. Hiking in autumn ❶ is wonderful, doesn't it? I found many colorful leaves on the ground. ❷ How beautiful were the colors! At that time, I found a squirrel. The squirrel didn't see me because it was eating an acorn. ❸ What a squirrel cute! It ❹ was an interesting experience, was it?

❶ _____ is wonderful, isn't it? _____   ❷ _____

❸ _____   ❹ _____

Words **wide** (폭이) 넓은 **perfect** 완벽한 **hero** 영웅 **special** 특별한 **recipe** 요리법
autumn 가을 **find** 찾다, 발견하다 (과거형 **found**) **colorful** (색이) 다채로운
ground 땅, 지면 **squirrel** 다람쥐 **acorn** 도토리 **experience** 경험

Wrap-Up Test

[1-2] 빈칸에 알맞은 말이 바르게 짝지어진 것을 고르세요.

1.

> • Jane can't play the piano, _____?
> • They went shopping, _____?

① can she – did they
② does she – do they
③ can she – didn't they
④ can't she – didn't they
⑤ can't she – did they

2.

> • _____ thick the book is!
> • _____ a delicious cake it is!
> • He looks mad at you, _____?

① How – What – does he
② What – How – does he
③ How – How – doesn't he
④ What – What – doesn't he
⑤ How – What – doesn't he

3. 빈칸에 들어갈 수 <u>없는</u> 것을 고르세요.

> _____, didn't he?

① He lost the race
② He did his best
③ He had dinner with you
④ He was born in Seoul
⑤ He had an appointment

4. 밑줄 친 부분을 바르게 고친 것을 고르세요.

> • What <u>interesting</u> story it is!
> • Daniel was so lazy, <u>isn't he</u>?

① How interesting – is he
② How interesting – wasn't he
③ What an interesting – was he
④ What an interesting – wasn't he
⑤ What interesting an – was he

Words　　thick 두꺼운　　mad 몹시 화가 난　　race 경주, 시합　　be born 태어나다
appointment 약속

5. 빈칸에 알맞은 말을 써서 부가의문문을 완성하세요.

> Sally told you that story, _____ _____?

[6-8] 우리말을 영어로 바르게 옮긴 것을 고르세요.

6.

> 그녀는 정말 사랑스러워!

① How lovely she is!
② How a lovely she is!
③ What lovely she is!
④ What a lovely she is!
⑤ How lovely is she!

7.

> 이곳은 안전한 장소가 아니에요, 그렇죠?

① This is not a safe place, is it?
② This is a safe place, isn't it?
③ This is a safe place, is it?
④ This is not a safe place, it is?
⑤ This is not a safe place, isn't it?

8.

> 그는 정말 인기 있는 가수야!

① What he is a popular singer!
② What popular a singer he is!
③ What a popular singer is he!
④ What a popular singer he is!
⑤ What he is popular a singer!

9. 빈칸에 들어갈 말이 나머지와 <u>다른</u> 것을 고르세요.

① _____ cool it is!
② _____ a smart boy!
③ _____ cute the kitten is!
④ _____ bright the moon is!
⑤ _____ exciting the roller coaster is!

[10-11] 틀린 문장을 고르세요.

10.

① How different!
② What large boxes!
③ What amazing score!
④ How hard the work is!
⑤ What terrible soup it is!

 Words   **place** 장소   **kitten** 아기 고양이   **bright** 밝은   **roller coaster** 롤러코스터
different 다른   **score** 점수   **hard** 어려운   **terrible** 끔찍한   **soup** 수프

11.

① Karen is your sister, isn't she?

② He can't play tennis, can he?

③ It'll rain tomorrow, won't it?

④ David gave you a letter, doesn't he?

⑤ You were busy yesterday, weren't you?

12. 대화가 <u>어색한</u> 것을 고르세요.

① A: How sad!

　B: I think so, too.

② A: What a wonderful day!

　B: Let's go for a walk.

③ A: You will watch the game, won't you?

　B: No, I didn't.

④ A: Mike broke the window, didn't he?

　B: Yes, he did. He's in trouble.

⑤ A: He should clean the room, shouldn't he?

　B: You are right. He must do it.

서술형
13. 두 문장이 비슷한 의미가 되도록 빈칸에 알맞은 말을 쓰세요.

> What a pretty dress it is!
>
> = How ＿＿＿＿＿＿＿＿＿＿＿＿＿＿！

서술형
[14-15] 우리말과 같은 뜻이 되도록 주어진 말을 이용하여 문장을 완성하세요.

14.

> 그건 정말 멋진 그림이다! (it, nice, picture)

➜ ＿＿＿＿＿＿＿＿＿＿＿＿＿＿＿＿

15.

> 너는 약속을 지킬 수 있지, 그렇지 않니?
>
> (keep your promise)

➜ ＿＿＿＿＿＿＿＿＿＿＿＿＿＿＿＿

＿＿＿＿＿＿＿＿＿＿＿＿＿＿＿＿

 Words   **I think so, too.** 나도 그렇게 생각해.   **be in trouble** 곤경에 처하다   **keep a promise** 약속을 지키다

UNIT 10

부정의문문

선택의문문

🫘 **Vocab Check!** 이번 과에서 배울 단어의 뜻을 확인하고, 모르는 단어에 체크 표시하세요.

✓ **1** prefer	图 선호하다	**11** classical	图 고전의, 고전적인	**21** mistake	명 실수
2 lock	图 잠그다	**12** city	명 도시	**22** still	부 아직
3 for free	무료로, 공짜로	**13** noisy	图 시끄러운	**23** writer	명 작가
4 beef	명 소고기	**14** violent	图 폭력적인	**24** club activity	동아리 활동
5 pork	명 돼지고기	**15** ship	명 배	**25** drawing	명 그림
6 mystery novel	명 추리 소설	**16** leave	图 떠나다; 남기다	**26** show	图 보여주다
7 pop music	명 대중음악	**17** both of	둘 다	**27** flavor	명 맛, 풍미
8 seat	명 좌석, 자리	**18** message	명 메시지	**28** scissors	명 가위
9 poster	명 포스터, 벽보	**19** sold out	매진된, 다 팔린	**29** green tea	명 녹차
10 seafood	명 해산물	**20** glue	명 풀	**30** cost	图 (돈이) 들다

부정의문문과 선택의문문

A: Which do you prefer, cake or ice cream?
당신은 케이크와 아이스크림 중 어떤 것을 더 좋아해요?

B: I like ice cream better. Isn't it so sweet?
나는 아이스크림을 더 좋아해요. 정말 달콤하지 않나요?

A: Yes, it is! 네, 달콤해요!

 부정의문문

부정의문문은 '~하지 않니?'처럼 부정으로 묻는 말이에요. 의문문 맨 앞에 나오는 be동사, do, 조동사에 not이 더해져 부정형으로 시작해요.

	어순	
be동사	**Isn't / Aren't** (현재) **Wasn't / Weren't** (과거)	+ 주어 ~?
do / does / did	**Don't / Doesn't** (현재) **Didn't** (과거)	+ 주어 + 동사원형 ~?
조동사	**Can't / Won't**	

부정의문문도 부가의문문처럼 대답의 내용이 긍정이면 yes, 부정이면 no를 써서 답해요.

Aren't they famous singers?
– **Yes**, they **are**. They're very famous in Korea.

Didn't he write this comic book?
– **No**, he **didn't** write it.

Can't you see stars in the sky?
– **Yes**. There are a lot of stars in the sky.

> 부정의문문에서 동사의
> 부정형은 줄임말로 써요.
> Isn't it your hat? (O)
> Is not it your hat? (X)

B 선택의문문

선택의문문은 말 그대로 두 가지 중 어떤 것을 선택할지 물어보는 말이에요. 접속사 or를 써서 선택지를 제시해요. 선택의문문에 대답할 때는 yes나 no를 쓰지 않고, 제시된 것 중 하나를 골라서 말해야 해요.

종류	어순
의문사가 없는 선택의문문	동사 + 주어 + A or B?
의문사가 있는 선택의문문	Which (+명사) / Who + 동사 + 주어 ~, A or B?

Do you want coffee? + Do you want tea?

⇨ Do you want coffee or tea?
– I want tea.

Are they brothers? + Are they friends?

⇨ Are they brothers or friends?
– They are friends.

Which color do you like better, black or white?
– I like white better.

Who is taller, you or your sister?
– My sister is taller.

> which(어느 (것))는 사물,
> who(누구)는 사람에 대해
> 말할 때 써요.

🍌 My Grammar Notes

1 부정의문문: ~하지 않니?

_____ _____ pretty? (그녀는 예쁘지 않니?)

_____ _____ like pizza? (너는 피자를 좋아하지 않니?)

_____ _____ play the drums? (너는 드럼을 칠 수 있지 않니?)

2 선택의문문: _____를 써서 어느 한쪽의 선택을 요구하는 의문문

(1) 의문사가 없을 때: Does she need a pen _____ a notebook?

(2) 의문사가 있을 때: _____ do you want, rice _____ bread?

_____ ate the chocolate, Hana _____ Doona?

Warm-Up

A ( ) 안에서 알맞은 것을 고르세요. 부정의문문

1. (Isn't / Doesn't) she like sports?

2. (Isn't / Doesn't) it a beautiful day?

3. (Aren't / Don't) you hungry now?

4. (Aren't / Don't) you enjoy waffle?

5. (Isn't / Doesn't) he your brother?

6. (Aren't / Don't) you remember me?

7. (Aren't / Don't) they your friends?

8. (Weren't / Didn't) you bring your umbrella?

B 빈칸에 알맞은 말을 써서 대답을 완성하세요. 부정의문문

1. Isn't this your painting?　　　　– 　Yes　, it is.

2. Aren't these their seats?　　　– Yes, 　　　　　　.

3. Didn't I lock the door?　　　　– 　　　　, you did.

4. Can't you open the window?　　– No, 　　　　　　.

5. Didn't he make the movie poster? – No, 　　　　　　.

6. Doesn't she work at the office?　– Yes, 　　　　　　.

7. Didn't you finish your homework? – 　　　　, I didn't.

8. Didn't they study together?　　　– 　　　　, they did.

C ( ) 안에서 알맞은 것을 고르세요. 선택의문문

1. ((Do) / Which) you like singing or dancing?

2. (Do / Which) came first, the chicken or the egg?

3. Which do you want for dinner, beef (and / or) pork?

4. (Who / Which) gave you this book, Cindy or David?

5. Do you prefer to go to a movie (and / or) go shopping?

6. (Who / Which) do you like better, romance novels or mystery novels?

Words

beef 소고기
pork 돼지고기
prefer 선호하다
romance novel 연애 소설
mystery novel 추리 소설
pop music 대중음악
gym 체육관
classical 고전의, 고전적인

D 질문에 알맞은 대답을 보기에서 고르세요. 선택의문문

보기   ⓐ I like pop music.   ⓑ I like the color red.

ⓒ She is a doctor.   ⓓ I will go to the gym.

ⓔ The black one is his.   ⓕ James is taller than Mike.

1. Is she a doctor or a nurse?   ⓒ

2. Who is taller, James or Mike?

3. Will you go to the library or the gym?

4. Which color do you like, red or blue?

5. Do you like classical music or pop music?

6. Which is his car, the black one or the blue one?

Practice

A 빈칸에 알맞은 말을 써서 부정의문문을 완성하세요.

1. They are happy. → **Aren't** **they** happy?

2. He loves her. → _____ _____ love her?

3. It is cold here. → _____ _____ cold here?

4. I can leave a message. → _____ _____ leave a message?

5. The pasta was delicious. → _____ the pasta delicious?

6. Chris wore new jeans. → _____ _____ wear new jeans?

B 빈칸에 알맞은 말을 보기에서 고르세요.

보기
ⓐ English or Spanish
ⓑ by bus or on foot
ⓒ coffee or green tea
ⓓ swimming or jogging
ⓔ Germany or England
ⓕ today or tomorrow

1. How do you get to school, **ⓑ** ?

2. Does he speak _____ ?

3. Which exercise do you like better, _____ ?

4. Which do you want to drink, _____ ?

5. Are you going to see the doctor _____ ?

6. Which national team is going to win, _____ ?

Words

leave
떠나다; 남기다
message
메시지
pasta 파스타
delicious
맛있는
wear
입다, 착용하다
(과거형 **wore**)
jeans 청바지
Spanish
스페인어
on foot
걸어서, 도보로
green tea 녹차
Germany 독일
England
영국, 잉글랜드
national
국가의, 나라의

C 우리말과 같은 뜻이 되도록 빈칸에 알맞은 말을 쓰세요.

Words

think 생각하다
sold out
매진된, 다 팔린
gentle 다정한
boring 지루한
come along with
~와 함께 가다
for free
무료로, 공짜로

1. 너는 배고프지 않니?

➔   Aren't   you   hungry?

2. 너는 그렇게 생각하지 않니?

➔   think so?

3. 그 장난감은 다 팔리지 않았니?

➔   the toy sold out?

4. 너는 우유와 주스 중에 어떤 것을 샀니?

➔   did you buy, milk   juice?

5. 그는 집에 운전해서 가니, 아니면 버스를 타니?

➔   he drive home   take the bus?

6. Mike와 Jack 중 누가 더 다정하니?

➔   gentler, Mike   Jack?

7. Ted는 공부를 하고 있니, 아니면 TV를 보고 있니?

➔   Ted studying   watching TV?

8. 이 영화는 지루하지 않았니? – 응, 지루했어.

➔   this movie boring? –   , it   .

9. 너는 나와 함께 갈 수 없니? – 아니, 갈 수 없어.

➔   come along with me?

     –   , I   .

10. 너는 그 표를 공짜로 얻지 않았니? – 응, 그랬어.

➔   get the ticket for free?

     – Yes,   did.

D 빈칸에 알맞은 말을 넣어 대화를 완성하세요.

Words

cloudy 흐린, 구름이 낀
favorite 가장 좋아하는
ship 배
need 필요하다
cream 크림
sell 팔다
both of 둘 다
club activity 동아리 활동
after school 방과 후에
city 도시
visit 방문하다
subject 과목

1. A: Didn't __you__ like the movie?

   B: __Yes__ , I __did__ . It was awesome.

2. A: Isn't it cloudy today?

   B: _____ , _____ . It is sunny.

3. A: Isn't Tom's favorite color blue?

   B: _____ , _____ . He really likes it.

4. A: Can't she come to the party?

   B: _____ , _____ . She is busy.

5. A: _____ he go to Japan by plane _____ by ship?

   B: He went there by plane.

6. A: _____ you need, sugar _____ cream?

   B: I need sugar.

7. A: _____ the shop sell clothes _____ shoes?

   B: It sells both of them.

8. A: Doesn't he do club activities after school?

   B: _____ , _____ . He doesn't like them.

9. A: _____ city did you visit, New York _____ Chicago?

   B: I visited New York.

10. A: _____ your favorite subject, English

    _____ math?

    B: I don't like any of them.

E 빈칸에 공통으로 알맞은 말을 고르세요.

Words

hair 머리카락
comic book 만화책
funny 재미있는
pants 바지
trip 여행
cost (돈이) 들다
throw ~ a surprise party ~에게 깜짝파티를 열어주다

1. _____ do you prefer, long hair or short hair?

_____ is your favorite subject, math or science?

✓① Which   ② Who   ③ How

2. _____ called you last night?

_____ is your best friend, Harry or Ron?

① Which   ② Who   ③ What

3. _____ you come earlier? – No, I _____ .

① Can[can]   ② Can't[can't]   ③ Aren't[aren't]

4. _____ the baby crying? – No, he _____ .

① Did[did]   ② Didn't[didn't]   ③ Isn't[isn't]

F 밑줄 친 부분을 바르게 고쳐 쓰세요.

1. <u>Doesn't</u> the comic book funny?   →

2. <u>Who</u> do you want, a skirt or pants?   →

3. Will you leave here today <u>but</u> tomorrow?   →

4. <u>Aren't</u> a trip to Europe cost a lot?   →

5. Which color do you like, red <u>and</u> yellow?   →

6. Who did you meet, Mr. Park <u>and</u> Mr. Lee?   →

7. Don't you throw her a surprise party?   →
– Yes, I <u>don't</u>.

A 우리말과 같은 뜻이 되도록 주어진 말을 바르게 배열하세요.

1. 너는 해산물을 좋아하지 않니? (you / seafood / like / don't)

   → _____ Don't you like seafood? _____

2. 그녀가 사실을 말하지 않았니? (tell / she / didn't / the truth)

   → _____

3. 너는 학교에 버스를 타고 가니, 아니면 지하철을 타니?
   (you / do / by bus / by subway / go to school / or)

   → _____

4. Emma와 Olivia 중 누가 네 여자친구니?
   (is / your girlfriend / Emma / who / or / Olivia)

   → _____

5. 여름과 겨울 중 어느 계절을 더 좋아하니?
   (which / do / summer / winter / you / season / like / better / or)

   → _____

B 우리말과 같은 뜻이 되도록 주어진 말을 이용하여 문장을 만드세요.

1. 1) 너는 생선을 못 먹니? (can)

   → __Can't__ you eat fish?

   2) 그는 당근을 못 먹니? (can, eat carrots)

   → _____ Can't he eat carrots? _____

2. 1) 너 학교에 늦은 거 아니니?

   → _____ you late for school?

2) 그녀는 너에게 관심 있는 거 아니니? (interested in)

→ _____

3. 1) 가위와 풀 중 너는 어떤 것이 필요하니?

→ _____ do you need, scissors _____ glue?

2) 치즈와 버터 중 너는 어떤 것을 원하니? (want, cheese, butter)

→ _____

4. 1) Daniel과 Julien 중에 누가 그 경기에서 이겼니?

→ _____ won the game, Daniel _____ Julien?

2) 너와 Jessica 중에 누가 그 나무를 심었니? (plant the tree)

→ _____

C 다음 대화를 읽고, 밑줄 친 부분을 바르게 고쳐 쓰세요.

A: ❶ <u>Whose do you like better</u>, football or soccer?

B: Football! ❷ <u>Weren't it exciting?</u> It's speedy. The rules are simple.

A: I don't think so. I think soccer is better. Football is violent.

B: Okay. Let's stop. ❸ <u>Don't you wanting some water?</u> I'm thirsty.

A: Good idea. Don't you like coffee now?

B: ❹ <u>No, I don't.</u> I want iced latte.

↓

❶ ___Which do you like better___   ❷ _____

❸ _____   ❹ _____

Words seafood 해산물   truth 사실   carrot 당근   interested in ~에 관심이 있는
scissors 가위   glue 풀   plant (나무를) 심다   speedy 빠른   rule 규칙
simple 간단한   violent 폭력적인   thirsty 목마른   iced 차게 식힌; 얼음을 넣은

Wrap-up Test

[1-2] 다음 문장을 부정의문문으로 바르게 바꾼 것을 고르세요.

1.

> It is your mistake.

① Is it your mistake?

② Isn't it your mistake?

③ Is not it your mistake?

④ It is your mistake, isn't it?

⑤ It isn't your mistake, is it?

2.

> She still works there.

① Is she still work there?

② Isn't she still work there?

③ Does she still work there?

④ Doesn't she still work there?

⑤ Does not she still works there?

[3-5] 빈칸에 알맞은 것을 고르세요.

3.

> A: _____ you have any money?
>
> B: No, I don't.

① Aren't   ② Weren't   ③ Don't

④ Didn't   ⑤ Doesn't

4.

> A: Isn't he a famous writer?
>
> B: _____ He's very
>
>   famous in the U.S.

① Yes, he is.   ② No, he isn't.

③ Yes, he does.   ④ No, he doesn't.

⑤ Yes, he was.

5.

> A: _____ animals do you like better,
>
>   cats or dogs?
>
> B: I like cats better.

① Who   ② Which   ③ How

④ Why   ⑤ When

 Words   **mistake** 실수   **still** 아직   **writer** 작가   **animal** 동물

6. 빈칸에 알맞은 말이 바르게 짝지어진 것을 고르세요.

> • _____ he go to school yesterday?
>
> • Which do you want, milk _____ juice?

① Isn't – and
② Wasn't – or
③ Doesn't – and
④ Didn't – or
⑤ Don't – but

7. 질문에 대한 대답으로 알맞은 것을 고르세요.

> A: Can't you show me your drawings?
> B: _____

① No, I can. Here they are.
② Yes. I don't want to show you.
③ Yes, I can't. I am not good at drawing.
④ Yes, I did. I showed my drawings to you.
⑤ No. I will show them to you when I finish.

8. 우리말을 영어로 바르게 옮긴 것을 고르세요.

> 내가 너에게 그에 대해 말하지 않았니?

① Did I tell you about him?
② Didn't I tell you about him?
③ Can't I tell you about him?
④ Did not tell you about him?
⑤ Did not I tell you about him?

9. 빈칸에 **Which**가 들어갈 수 <u>없는</u> 것을 고르세요.

① _____ do you like better, history or math?
② _____ book are you looking for?
③ _____ are you friends or sisters?
④ _____ do you want, tea or coffee?
⑤ _____ food will you eat, chicken or beef?

10. <u>틀린</u> 문장을 고르세요.

① Didn't he bring his car?
② Won't they give you a gift?
③ Aren't you help your parents?
④ Who will come here, Amy or Cathy?
⑤ Which flavor do you like, chocolate or caramel?

Words show 보여주다 **drawing** 그림 **be good at** ~을 잘하다 **gift** 선물 **flavor** 맛, 풍미

11. 대화가 <u>어색한</u> 것을 고르세요.

① A: Didn't you eat breakfast?

　B: Yes, I had breakfast.

② A: Isn't he your boyfriend?

　B: No, he is my brother.

③ A: Can't you speak English?

　B: Yes. I can speak Chinese, too.

④ A: Which country did you visit, Japan or China?

　B: Yes, I did.

⑤ A: Who works better, John or Mina?

　B: Both work well.

서술형

12. 다음 문장을 부정의문문으로 고치고, 대답을 완성하세요.

> You like macarons.

➔ _____ _____ _____

　macarons?

– _____, _____ _____.

　I love French desserts.

서술형

13. 우리말과 같은 뜻이 되도록 주어진 말을 이용하여 문장을 완성하세요.

> 햄버거와 샌드위치 중 어떤 것을 원하니?
> (which, want, a hamburger, a sandwich)

➔ _____

　_____

14. 우리말과 같은 뜻이 되도록 주어진 말을 바르게 배열하세요.

> Jason과 Lily 중 누가 널 기다렸니?
> (you / Jason / waited for / Lily / who)

➔ _____

　_____

서술형

15. 밑줄 친 부분을 바르게 고쳐 쓰세요.

> A: Can't you come back on the weekend?
> B: <u>Yes, I can.</u> I am very busy then.

➔ _____

**Words**　　**country** 나라　　**macaron** 마카롱　　**French** 프랑스의　　**dessert** 후식, 디저트

sandwich 샌드위치　　**busy** 바쁜

부록

1

비교급과 최상급		

원급		비교급	최상급
대부분의 형용사/부사		원급 + er	원급 + est
old	나이가 많은	older	oldest
long	긴	longer	longest
fast	빠른	faster	fastest
tall	(키가) 큰	taller	tallest
smart	영리한	smarter	smartest
young	젊은, 어린	younger	youngest
-e로 끝날 때		원급 + r	원급 + st
nice	멋진	nicer	nicest
wise	현명한	wiser	wisest
large	(크기가) 큰	larger	largest
-y로 끝날 때		y를 i로 바꾸고 + er	y를 i로 바꾸고 + est
happy	행복한	happier	happiest
busy	바쁜	busier	busiest
pretty	예쁜	prettier	prettiest
easy	쉬운	easier	easiest
heavy	무거운	heavier	heaviest
'모음 1개+자음 1개'로 끝날 때		자음 한 번 더 + er	자음 한 번 더 + est
big	(크기가) 큰	bigger	biggest
hot	뜨거운	hotter	hottest
fat	뚱뚱한	fatter	fattest
thin	마른	thinner	thinnest
일부 2음절 또는 3음절 단어		more + 원급	most + 원급
famous	유명한	more famous	most famous
beautiful	아름다운	more beautiful	most beautiful
important	중요한	more important	most important
popular	인기 있는	more popular	most popular

carefully	조심스럽게	more carefully	most carefully
interesting	흥미로운	more interesting	most interesting
불규칙적인 형태			
good/well	좋은/잘	better	best
bad	나쁜	worse	worst
little	조금, 약간	less	least
many/much	많은	more	most

2 ◀ to부정사와 동명사를 목적어로 취하는 동사

to부정사를 목적어로 취하는 동사

agree	동의하다	fail	실패하다	prepare	준비하다
ask	부탁하다	help	돕다	promise	약속하다
choose	선택하다	hope	희망하다	seem	~처럼 보이다
decide	결정하다	learn	배우다	want	원하다
expect	기대하다	plan	계획하다	wish	바라다

동명사를 목적어로 취하는 동사

avoid	피하다	finish	끝내다	suggest	제안하다
enjoy	즐기다	mind	꺼리다	give up	포기하다

to부정사와 동명사를 모두 목적어로 취하는 동사

begin	시작하다	like	좋아하다	remember	기억하다
start	시작하다	love	사랑하다	forget	잊다

전치사

for	~을 위해 (목적)
	~을 향하여 (방향)
	~의 대가로
	~을 이유로
	~치고는, ~에 비해서는
	~에 찬성하여
by	~의 곁에
	~에 의해 (행위자)
	~함으로써 (방법)
	~을 타고 (교통수단)
	~까지
at	~에서 (장소, 지점)
	~한 시각에, 시점에
	~한 상태에 있는
	~으로 인하여 (원인)
in	~ 안에
	~ 후에
	~을 입고 있는
	~한 상태에 있는
to	~에, ~으로 (목적지)
	~ 전 (시각)
	~하게도 (감정)
about	~에 관하여
above	~의 위에, ~보다 높이
along	~을 따라
in front of	~의 앞에
next to	~의 옆에
during	~동안
within	(일정한 기간) ~이내에
after	~후에
past	~지나서

on	~의 표면에, 위에
	(특정한) ~때에
	~에 관한, ~에 대한
	~하자마자
	~으로 (수단)
	~을 근거로, 이유로
of	~의 (소유)
	~로 인해 (원인)
	~으로 만든 (재료)
	~에 대한
with	~와 함께
	~을 가지고 (도구)
	~ 때문에 (원인)
	~한 채로
from	~에서, ~로부터 (출발점)
	~로 인해 (원인)
	~로 (성분, 재료)
	~을 못하도록 (금지)
out of	~의 밖으로
	~로 (재료)
across	~을 가로질러
under	~의 바로 아래
between	(두 가지 대상) ~의 사이에
behind	~의 뒤에
toward	~을 향해, ~쪽으로
around	~주위에
through	~동안 내내
until / till	~까지 (계속)
before	~전에

4

and	그리고	when	~할 때, ~할 때마다
but	그러나	while	~하는 동안에, ~하면서
or	또는	as	~할 때, ~함에 따라
so	그래서	until	~할 때까지 (계속)
after	~ 후에	by the time	~할 때까지 (완료)
before	~ 전에	since	~한 이래로
as long as	~하는 한	because	~이기 때문에
both A and B	A와 B 둘 다	if	만일 ~라면
either A or B	A 또는 B	unless	만일 ~가 아니라면
neither A nor B	A와 B 둘 다 아닌	though	비록 ~이지만
not only A but also B	A뿐만 아니라 B 또한	in case	~의 경우에 대비하여

지은이

NE능률 영어교육연구소

NE능률 영어교육연구소는 혁신적이며 효율적인 영어 교재를 개발하고
영어 학습의 질을 한 단계 높이고자 노력하는 NE능률의 연구조직입니다.

Grammar Bean 4

펴 낸 이 주민홍
펴 낸 곳 서울특별시 마포구 월드컵북로 396(상암동) 누리꿈스퀘어 비즈니스타워 10층
㈜NE능률 (우편번호 03925)
펴 낸 날 2019년 1월 5일 개정판 제1쇄 발행
2024년 3월 15일 제9쇄
전   화 02 2014 7114
팩   스 02 3142 0356
홈페이지 www.neungyule.com
등록번호 제1-68호
I S B N 979-11-253-2488-1 63740
정   가 12,000원

NE 능률

고객센터

교재 내용 문의 : contact.nebooks.co.kr (별도의 가입 절차 없이 작성 가능)
제품 구매, 교환, 불량, 반품 문의 : 02-2014-7114
☎ 전화문의는 본사 업무시간 중에만 가능합니다.

GRAMMAR

BEAN

Workbook 4

GRAMMAR
BEAN

—•— 그래머빈 —•—

4 Workbook

NE능률 교재 MAP

아래 교재 MAP을 참고하여 본인의 현재 혹은 목표 수준에 따라 교재를 선택하세요.
NE능률 교재들과 함께 영어실력을 쑥쑥~ 올려보세요!
MP3 등 교재 부가 학습 서비스 및 자세한 교재 정보는 www.nebooks.co.kr 에서 확인하세요.

문법
구문

초1-2	초3	초3-4	초4-5	초5-6
	그래머버디 1	그래머버디 2	그래머버디 3	Grammar Bean 3
	초등영어 문법이 된다 Starter 1	초등영어 문법이 된다 Starter 2	Grammar Bean 1	Grammar Bean 4
		초등 Grammar Inside 1	Grammar Bean 2	초등영어 문법이 된다 2
		초등 Grammar Inside 2	초등영어 문법이 된다 1	초등 Grammar Inside 5
			초등 Grammar Inside 3	초등 Grammar Inside 6
			초등 Grammar Inside 4	

초6-예비중	중1	중1-2	중2-3	중3
능률중학영어 예비중	능률중학영어 중1	능률중학영어 중2	Grammar Zone 기초편	능률중학영어 중3
Grammar Inside Starter	Grammar Zone 입문편	1316 Grammar 2	Grammar Zone 워크북 기초편	문제로 마스터하는 중학영문법 3
원리를 더한 영문법 STARTER	Grammar Zone 워크북 입문편	문제로 마스터하는 중학영문법 2	1316 Grammar 3	Grammar Inside 3
	1316 Grammar 1	Grammar Inside 2	원리를 더한 영문법 2	열중 16강 문법 3
	문제로 마스터하는 중학영문법 1	열중 16강 문법 2	중학영문법 총정리 모의고사 2	중학영문법 총정리 모의고사 3
	Grammar Inside 1	원리를 더한 영문법 1	쓰기로 마스터하는 중학서술형 2학년	쓰기로 마스터하는 중학서술형 3학년
	열중 16강 문법 1	중학영문법 총정리 모의고사 1	중학 천문장 3	
	쓰기로 마스터하는 중학서술형 1학년	중학 천문장 2		
	중학 천문장 1			

예비고-고1	고1	고1-2	고2-3	고3
문제로 마스터하는 고등영문법	Grammar Zone 기본편 1	필히 통하는 고등 영문법 실력편	Grammar Zone 종합편	
올클 수능 어법 start	Grammar Zone 워크북 기본편 1	필히 통하는 고등 서술형 실전편	Grammar Zone 워크북 종합편	
천문장 입문	Grammar Zone 기본편 2	TEPS BY STEP G+R Basic	올클 수능 어법 완성	
	Grammar Zone 워크북 기본편 2		천문장 완성	
	필히 통하는 고등 영문법 기본편			
	필히 통하는 고등 서술형 기본편			
	천문장 기본			

수능 이상/ 토플 80-89· 텝스 600-699점	수능 이상/ 토플 90-99· 텝스 700-799점	수능 이상/ 토플 100· 텝스 800점 이상		
TEPS BY STEP G+R 1	TEPS BY STEP G+R 2	TEPS BY STEP G+R 3		

GRAMMAR

BEAN

정답 및 해설 4

 **UNIT 01** 비교급과 최상급

B Mike는 나보다 키가 더 커요.

캐나다는 미국보다 더 커요.

여름은 봄보다 더 더워요.

그녀는 나보다 더 주의 깊게 운전해요.

C Adams 선생님은 우리 학교에서 최고의 선생님이에요.

Tony는 그의 반에서 가장 빨리 달려요.

1월은 일 년 중 가장 추운 달이에요.

그는 한국에서 가장 유명한 배우예요.

🫘 My Grammar Notes   p.9

1. more beautiful, busier

2. largest, saddest 3. than 4. the

Step1 Warm-Up   p.10-11

A 1. longer 2. biggest 3. smaller

4. better 5. cheapest 6. most famous

7. taller-tallest 8. younger-youngest

9. more-most 10. heavier-heaviest

11. faster-fastest

12. more interesting – most interesting

13. larger – largest 14. worse – worst

15. more popular – most popular

16. happier – happiest

17. more expensive – most expensive

18. sadder – saddest

B 1. ○ 2. V 3. ○ 4. ○ 5. V 6. ○ 7. V

8. V

C 1. smaller 2. tallest 3. older

4. hottest 5. more important

6. easiest 7. less 8. laziest

Step2 Practice   p.12-15

A 1. higher 2. the most expensive

3. safer 4. the happiest 5. the richest

6. shorter 7. more famous

8. the most popular 9. the youngest

10. slower 11. the best

12. the longest 13. the funniest

14. easier 15. the worst

16. the fastest 17. the most difficult

18. the most interesting

B 1. 1) taller than 2) shorter than

3) the tallest

2. 1) younger than 2) older than

3) the youngest

3. 1) cheaper than

2) more expensive than

3) the most expensive

C 1. 1) long 2) longer

2. 1) clean 2) cleanest

3. 1) sad 2) saddest

4. 1) faster 2) fastest

5. 1) beautiful 2) most beautiful

D 1. slower than 2. bigger than

3. larger than 4. the most popular

5. the best 6. worse than

7. more important

E 1. the laziest 2. faster than

3. lighter than 4. the youngest

5. hotter than 6. more difficult than

7. the cheapest 8. better than

9. the longest 10. the most important

11. the coziest

Step3 Grammar into Writing

p.16-17

A
1. is colder than fall
2. is smaller than Jeju Island
3. is the largest country
4. is the highest mountain

B
1. is younger than David
2. is taller than Billy
3. is heavier than the box of kiwis

C
1. My room is darker than your room.
2. Who is the richest person in the world?
3. He was the bravest of all the soldiers.
4. Today is warmer than yesterday.

D
1. the most beautiful   2. the prettiest
3. prettier than

Wrap-Up Test

p.18-20

1. ④   2. ③   3. ①   4. ④   5. ②   6. ①
7. ②   8. ④   9. ③   10. ③   11. ②
12. I'm the shortest student in my class.   13. higher than   14. get up later than   15. more, than

1. ①②③⑤는 모두 -er을 붙여 비교급을 만들지만, ④ expensive는 앞에 more를 붙여서 만든다.
2. ③ good – better – best / bad – worse – worst
3. 앞에 more가 있으므로, smarter는 들어갈 수 없다.
4. 최상급 표현은 'the＋최상급＋in/of ~'의 어순을 취하며, high는 1음절 단어이므로 끝에 est를 붙여 최상급 형태를 만든다.
5. 의미상 '~에서(장소)'를 뜻하는 in이 알맞다. of는 '~ 중에서'를 뜻한다.
6. the＋최상급＋of ~: ~ 중에서 가장 …한
7. 첫 번째 문장에는 than이 쓰였으므로 형용사의 비교급을 써야 하고, 두 번째 문장은 'the＋최상급＋in'의 어순을 따라 형용사의 최상급이 적절하다.
8. 첫 번째 빈칸에는 뒤에 than이 쓰였으므로 부사의 비교급이 들어가야 한다. 두 번째 빈칸에는 앞에 최상급 형태가, 뒤에 기간을 나타내는 the year가 쓰였으므로 '~ 중에서'라는 뜻의 of를 써야 한다.
9. ③ → I'm younger than Alice.
10. ③ heavyer → heavier
11. 뒤에 than이 나오므로 비교급이 되어야 한다. diligent의 비교급은 more diligent, warm의 비교급은 warmer이다.
12. the＋최상급＋in ~: ~에서 가장 …한
13. '높이'는 high로 표현하며, high의 비교급은 higher이다.
14. 내가 오빠보다 한 시간 더 늦게 일어나므로 비교급 later than을 이용해 문장을 완성한다.
15. Tom이 Jessie보다 2달러를 더 많이 가지고 있으므로, much의 비교급 more와 than을 이용해 문장을 완성한다.

UNIT 02 비교급과 최상급을 이용한 표현

A 기차는 버스보다 더 빨라요.
→ 비행기는 기차보다 훨씬 더 빨라요.
내 손은 언니의 손보다 더 커요.
→ 내 아버지의 손은 내 손보다 훨씬 더 커요.

B 나는 키가 점점 더 커지고 있어요.
날씨가 점점 더 추워지고 있어요.
영어는 점점 더 중요해지고 있어요.

C 더 많을수록, 더 좋다. (다다익선: 多多益善)
당신은 더 많이 가질수록, 더 많이 원하게 돼요.

나는 더 일찍 잠자리에 들수록, 더 일찍 일어나요.

가방이 더 클수록, 더 비싸요.

D 그것은 이 호텔에서 가장 좋은 방들 중 하나예요.

그들은 세계 최고의 밴드들 중 하나예요.

스티브 잡스는 세계에서 가장 유명한 최고경영자들 중 한 사람이었어요.

🫘 My Grammar Notes
p.23

1. much longer 2. and 3. the, the

4. one, one

Step1 Warm-Up
p.24-25

A 1. very 2. much 3. very 4. much

5. much 6. very

B 1. better 2. more

3. the more 4. warmer and warmer

5. more 6. worse and worse

C 1. one of the best 2. one of the largest

3. one of the smallest islands

4. one of the most famous actors

5. one of the happiest moments

D 1. faster 2. much faster 3. the fastest

4. slower 5. the slowest

Step2 Practice
p.26-29

A 1. 1) a√larger, much 2) a√large, very

2. 1) piano√well, very

   2) piano√better, much

3. 1) is√sweet, very

   2) is√sweeter, much

4. 1) is√tidy, very 2) is√tidier, much

B 1. darker, darker 2. better and better

3. fatter and fatter

4. more, more popular

C 1. ② 2. ③ 3. ③ 4. ② 5. ① 6. ④

D 1. ⓒ 2. ⓐ 3. ⓓ 4. ⓑ 5. ⓕ 6. ⓔ

E 1. 1) tall 2) much taller

2. 1) famous 2) more and more famous

3. 1) larger 2) the largest

4. 1) dangerous

   2) much more dangerous

5. 1) very difficult

   2) more and more difficult

   3) much more difficult

6. 1) the hottest 2) hotter and hotter

   3) much hotter

F 1. much smarter

2. weaker and weaker

3. the most popular

4. much more comfortable 5. the more

G 1. much 2. one of 3. more

4. much cuter 5. the longest rivers

6. the better 7. the loudest animals

Step3 Grammar into Writing
p.30-31

A 1. Brazil is larger than India.

2. China is much larger than India.

3. India is the smallest country of the three.

B 1. 1) much heavier than

   2) This book is much thicker than that book.

2. 1) smaller and smaller

   2) The earth is getting warmer and warmer.

3. 1) the highest

   2) A whale is one of the biggest animals in the world.

4. 1) much older than

2) My computer is much faster than yours[your computer].

5. 1) The more, the more

2) The more I learn, the more I forget.

C 1. the harder I practiced

2. the worse 3. much better

4. the best baseball players

Wrap-Up Test
p.32-34

1. ② **2.** ⑤ **3.** ④ **4.** ② **5.** ③ **6.** ⑤

7. shorter and shorter **8.** ① **9.** ⑤

10. ④ **11.** ④ **12.** ③

13. much smarter than

14. The faster the train runs, the earlier you can get there.

15. She is one of the most successful actresses

1. 비교급 앞에 much를 써서 비교급의 의미를 강조할 수 있다.

2. one of the＋최상급＋복수명사: 가장 ~한 …중 하나

3. the＋비교급, the＋비교급: ~할수록 점점 더 …하다

4. 비교급＋and＋비교급: 점점 더 ~한[하게] one of the＋최상급＋복수명사: 가장 ~한 …중 하나

5. careful의 비교급은 앞에 more를 붙여서 만든다. 비교급＋and＋비교급: 점점 더 ~한[하게]

6. 비교급을 강조할 때는 부사 much를 쓴다. the ＋비교급, the＋비교급: ~할수록 점점 더 …하다

7. 비교급＋and＋비교급: 점점 더 ~한[하게]

8. ① dark and dark → darker and darker

9. the＋비교급, the＋비교급: ~할수록 점점 더 …하다

10. one of the＋최상급＋복수명사: 가장 ~한 …중 하나

11. ④ 빈칸 앞에는 최상급이 쓰이고 뒤에는 집단(회사) 이 이어지므로 '~에서'의 의미인 in이 알맞다.

12. ③ very 다음에는 비교급을 쓸 수 없다.

13. 비교급을 강조할 때는 much(훨씬)를 쓴다.

14. the＋비교급, the＋비교급: ~할수록 점점 더 …하다

15. one of the＋최상급＋복수명사: 가장 ~한 …중 하나

UNIT 03 to부정사

B 나의 꿈은 가수가 되는 것이에요.

나는 쉬고 싶어요.

우리는 당신을 다시 보기를 바라요.

그는 체중을 줄이기로 결심했어요.

우리는 걸어서 인도를 여행할 계획을 짰어요.

그 과학자는 괴물을 만들어내는 것을 좋아해요.

C 일할 시간이에요.

저는 쓸 돈이 없어요.

당신은 마실 것을 원하나요?

그녀는 할 일이 많아요.

D 나는 그림을 그리려고 연필을 샀어요.

그녀는 영어를 공부하려고 캐나다에 갈 거예요.

그 아이들은 동물들을 보러 동물원에 갈 예정이에요.

My Grammar Notes
p.37

1. to **2.** 명사, to **3.** 형용사, to **4.** 부사, to

A 1. ○ 2. ○ 3. ✕ 4. ✕ 5. ○ 6. ✕ 7. ✕
8. ✕ 9. ○ 10. ○ 11. ✕ 12. ○ 13. ○
14. ✕ 15. ○ 16. ✕

B 1. 1) cooks 2) to cook
2. 1) to eat 2) eats
3. 1) to listen 2) listen
4. 1) got 2) to get
5. 1) to read 2) read

C 1. laundry ⓣo do
2. work ⓣo do
3. plans ⓣo go
4. the time ⓣo learn
5. nothing ⓣo eat
6. newspapers ⓣo read
7. clothes ⓣo wear

D 1. to be on time
2. to catch the train
3. to see a baseball game
4. to visit Canada
5. to buy some food
6. to take pictures

Step2 **Practice** p.40-43

A 1. likes ✓ swim
→ 그는 수영하는 것을 매우 좋아한다.
2. time ✓ say
→ 작별인사를 할 시간이다.
3. came ✓ see
→ 그녀는 어제 날 보러[보기 위해] 왔다.
4. decided ✓ be
→ 그는 과학자가 되기로 결심했다.
5. turn ✓ do
→ 설거지할 너의 차례야. / 네가 설거지할

차례야.
6. bakery ✓ buy
→ 나는 빵을 좀 사러[사기 위해] 제과점에 갔다.

B 1. to see 2. to arrive 3. to wake up
4. to pass 5. to visit 6. to fix

C 1. ⓐ 2. ⓑ 3. ⓑ 4. ⓐ 5. ⓐ 6. ⓒ
7. ⓑ 8. ⓐ 9. ⓒ 10. ⓒ 11. ⓐ 12. ⓒ
13. ⓑ 14. ⓒ 15. ⓒ 16. ⓑ 17. ⓐ
18. ⓒ

D 1. decided to keep 2. learn to swim
3. wanted to marry 4. began to clean
5. something to drink
6. time to exercise 7. nothing to say
8. money to take 9. a magazine to read
10. expect to hear

E 1. He came to the restaurant to eat
dinner.
2. We used the map to find the hotel.
3. I am going to the library to study for
my exam.
4. She went to the bathroom to wash
her hands.
5. She turned on the computer to play
games.

F 1. to know 2. to meet 3. to stay
4. to travel 5. to see 6. to visit
7. to walk

Step3 **Grammar into Writing** p.44-45

A 1. I hope to make foreign friends.
2. Andy plans to buy a new car.
3. My job is to translate foreign
languages.
4. We decided to move to another city.

B 1. 1) to lose weight

  2) Peter is saving to buy a bicycle.

 2. 1) to learn Japanese

  2) Mia went to New York to see musicals.

 3. 1) to fix my computer

  2) They are waiting for someone to fix their car.

 4. 1) to meet her friends

  2) Brian often goes home to take a nap.

C

I love to play soccer. Someday, I want to be a great soccer player. My dream is to win the World Cup. But I'm just a beginner right now. I need a coach to help me. I'll learn to kick the ball to get a goal!

나는 축구하는 것을 정말 좋아해요. 언젠가 나는 훌륭한 축구선수가 되고 싶어요. 내 꿈을 월드컵에서 우승하는 거예요. 하지만 나는 지금 그저 초보자예요. 나는 나를 도와줄 코치(감독)가 필요해요. 나는 골을 넣기 위해 공을 차는 것을 배울 거예요!

Wrap-Up Test
p.46~48

1. ④ 2. ④ 3. ④ 4. ① 5. ⑤ 6. ⑤

7. ④ 8. ② 9. ④ 10. ③ 11. ④

12. to make 13. Who was the first person to climb Mt. Everest?

14. My plan is to get there early.

15. I study hard to be a teacher.

1. 동사 hope 뒤에는 '~하는 것'의 의미로 명사처럼 쓰이는 to부정사가 와야 한다.

2. '~하기 위해'의 의미로 부사처럼 쓰이는 to부정사가 와야 한다.

3. decided의 목적어로 to부정사가 와야 하므로 빈칸에는 동사원형이 들어가야 한다.
   ④ saved → save

4. want의 목적어로는 to부정사나 명사가 올 수 있다.
   ① eat pizza → to eat pizza 또는 pizza

5. 각 빈칸에 '~하기 위해서'의 의미로 부사처럼 쓰이는 to부정사와 동사 wish의 목적어로 명사처럼 쓰이는 to부정사가 적절하다.

6. to부정사를 만들 때는 to 뒤에 동사원형을 쓴다.

7. ①②③⑤ ~하는 것(명사 역할), ④ ~할(형용사 역할)

8. ①③④⑤ ~하기 위해(부사 역할)
   ② ~하는 것(명사 역할)

9. want는 일반동사이므로 조동사 do를 써서 의문문을 만들어야 하며 want의 목적어로 to부정사가 와야 한다.

10. '사기 위해'의 의미로 부사처럼 쓰이는 to부정사 to buy가 와야 한다.

11. 의미상 '해야 할 숙제'라는 의미이므로 do 앞에 to를 써서 명사 homework를 꾸며주어야 한다.
   ④ do → to do

12. 의문사 Why를 사용해 이유를 묻고 있으므로, '~하기 위해'라는 부사처럼 쓰이는 to부정사를 이용해 대답해야 한다.

13. climb 앞에 to를 써서 형용사처럼 쓰이는 to부정사로 명사(the first person)를 꾸며 주어야 한다.

14. 'be동사+to부정사'의 형태로 '~은 …하는 것이다'의 의미로 be동사 뒤에 명사처럼 쓰이는 to부정사가 와야 한다.

15. '~하기 위해'의 의미로 부사처럼 쓰이는 to부정사가 와야 한다.

 **동명사**

B 그의 직업은 영어를 가르치는 것이에요.

그녀는 춤추는 것을 즐겨요.

우리는 숙제를 하는 것을 끝냈어요.

C 나는 조종사가 되고 싶어요.

우리는 우리 집을 팔기로 결심했어요.

그들은 뮤지컬 보는 것을 즐겨요.

당신은 편지 쓰는 것을 끝냈나요?

Jenny는 노래 부르는 것을 좋아해요.

🫘 My Grammar Notes p.51

1. -ing 2. 명사 3. is 4. to부정사, 동명사

Step1 Warm-Up p.52-53

A 1. reading 2. playing

3. Seeing, believing 4. listening

5. Speaking 6. Eating 7. Keeping

8. writing

B 1. 1) watching 2) watch

2. 1) tell 2) telling

3. 1) dances 2) dancing

4. 1) drives 2) driving

5. 1) playing 2) plays

C 1. ⓑ 2. ⓐ 3. ⓔ 4. ⓓ 5. ⓒ 6. ⓖ 7. ⓗ

8. ⓕ

D 1. talking 2. to go 3. taking, to take

4. to get 5. to meet

6. brushing, to brush

7. playing, to play 8. shopping, to shop

Step2 Practice p.54-57

A 1, 3, 6, 8

B 1. washing 2. is 3. walking

4. barking 5. is 6. watching

7. playing 8. is

C 1. eating 2. Learning 3. playing

4. reading 5. Traveling 6. Exercising

D 1. Climbing mountains

2. riding horses 3. taking photographs

4. running for an hour

5. playing soccer

6. smoking cigarettes

E 1. eating 2. watching 3. to meet

4. barking 5. to be 6. to cook

7. speaking 8. to stay

F 1. to see 2. fixing 3. isn't

4. reading 5. to speak 6. crying

7. making 8. waiting

G 1. want to stay 2. kept calling

3. hope to be 4. stopped smoking

5. finished making 6. enjoy relaxing

7. decided to learn 8. expected to see

9. gave up fixing 10. avoids eating

Step3 Grammar into Writing p.58-59

A 1. Learning a new language is

interesting.

2. Driving in the rain is not safe.

3. Becoming a famous actress is her

dream.

4. Getting up early is a good habit.

5. Wearing a tie is not healthy.

B 1. 1) buying

2) We gave up waiting for John.

  2. 1) smiling

    2) Jane kept asking the same question.

  3. 1) doing

    2) He finished writing a letter to Jake.

  4. 1) watching

    2) I avoid eating chicken late at night.

C **1.** is traveling **2.** hope to visit

  3. started to save / started saving

  4. Do you want to join me?

Wrap-Up Test

p.60-62

1. ② **2.** ② **3.** ④ **4.** ② **5.** ③ **6.** ④

7. ③ **8.** ⑤ **9.** ② **10.** ② **11.** ②

12. Sumin finished playing the guitar.

13. Speaking in English needs practice.

14. We gave up persuading Jack.

15. (1) I promised to go to the zoo.

(2) My dad quit drinking coffee.

1. many books를 목적어로 취하면서 문장의 주어 역할을 해야 하므로 동명사인 Reading이 알맞다.

2. decide, want, hope, promise 뒤에는 목적어로 to부정사를 써야 한다.

3. plan과 want 뒤에는 to부정사를, enjoy 뒤에는 동명사를 쓴다. like와 hate 뒤에는 to부정사와 동명사 모두 쓸 수 있다.

4. ② 동명사가 문장의 주어로 쓰일 때는 단수 취급한다.

5. ①②④⑤ 동명사, ③ 현재진행형

6. ①②③⑤ 진행형, ④ 동명사

7. keep 뒤에는 동명사를, promise 뒤에는 to부정사를 목적어로 쓴다.

8. avoid와 keep은 목적어로 동명사를, 동사 wish

는 목적어로 to부정사를 취한다.

9. ② seeing → to see

10. 문장의 주어는 Cleaning those rooms로, 동명사가 주어일 때 단수 취급한다.

② are → is

11. 운전하는 것을 멈췄다고 했으므로, stop 뒤에 목적어 역할을 하는 동명사 driving을 써야 한다. ①의 to drive는 '~하기 위해'의 의미로 부사처럼 쓰이는 to부정사이다.

12. finish 뒤에는 동명사를 쓴다.

13. 문장의 주어는 '영어로 말하는 것'이므로 동명사 (Speaking) 형태로 시작하고, 동명사는 단수 취급하므로 동사 자리에 needs가 이어지는 것이 알맞다.

14. give up은 목적어로 동명사를 취한다.

15. (1) promise는 목적어로 to부정사를 취한다.

(2) quit은 목적어로 동명사를 취한다.

UNIT 05 전치사 1 (장소, 위치)

B **1.** 우리는 런던에 있는 한 호텔에 머물렀어요.

그는 캐나다에 있는 한 공항에 있어요.

나는 그 식당에 있는 탁자에 앉았어요.

그들은 그 가게에 있는 계산대에 서 있었어요.

  2. 책상 위에 책 두 권이 있어요.

나의 고양이는 의자 아래에 있어요.

그녀는 내 앞에 앉아 있었어요.

한 소년이 나무 뒤에 숨어 있어요.

Kevin은 그 탁자를 창문 옆에 두었어요.

C 나는 Tony와 Mike 사이에 앉았어요.

여기서 박물관까지는 1킬로미터예요.

1. 전치사   2. 목적격, him   3. in, at, at, in

Step1 Warm-Up p.66-67

A 1. ⓓ 2. ⓒ 3. ⓑ 4. ⓐ 5. ⓔ

B 1. is√the sofa   2. stay√home
  3. Spanish√Mexico
  4. met√the fountain
  5. girl√the tree
  6. building√this street
  7. standing√Mike   8. guy√you
  9. travel√Paris

C 1. in 2. between 3. next to 4. on
  5. on 6. in 7. next to 8. on
  9. behind   10. in front of   11. between

Step2 Practice p.68-71

A 1. on 2. on 3. in 4. from 5. to
  6. next to 7. behind 8. between

B 1. in my pocket 2. at the bus stop
  3. in the sea 4. in the bottle
  5. in New York 6. at a hotel

C 1. in 2. on 3. under 4. in front of
  5. next to 6. from 7. between 8. at
  9. from   10. behind

D 1. on 2. in 3. at 4. under
  5. between, and 6. behind 7. in
  8. next to 9. in front of 10. from, to

E 1. in 2. on 3. me 4. at 5. at 6. in
  7. in front of

F 1. next to the bakery
  2. a lake behind my house
  3. a glass door in front of you
  4. from home to Seoul Tower

5. under my desk

Step3 Grammar into Writing p.72-73

A 1. Emily is sleeping on the sofa.
  2. I saw many stars in the sky.
  3. There are some toys under the closet.
  4. Who is the girl behind you in the
    picture?

B 1. 1) under the tree
    2) There are many fish under the sea.
  2. 1) in front of us 2) He is singing in
    front of many people.
  3. 1) between the earth and the moon
    2) What is the distance between
    Seoul and Tokyo?
  4. 1) next to my house
    2) The bookstore is next to my school.

C 1. behind the red car
  2. next to the church
  3. in front of the hospital
  4. between the hospital and the church

Wrap-Up Test p.74-76

1. ⑤ **2.** ② **3.** ③ **4.** ① **5.** ②
6. between, and **7.** from, to **8.** ③
9. ⑤ **10.** ④ **11.** ② **12.** ⑤ **13.** ⑤
14. He is standing in front of the
bookstore.
15. The bakery is behind the bank.

1. ⑤ in front of: ~ 앞에

2. 특정 지점을 가리킬 때는 전치사 at을 쓴다.

3. on: ~위에

4. 안팎이 명확히 구분되거나 국가·도시 등 넓은 장소

를 가리킬 때는 전치사 in을 쓴다.

5. ② 전치사 뒤에는 명사나 목적격 대명사가 온다.

6. between A and B: A와 B 사이에

7. from A to B: A에서 B까지

8. next to: ~ 옆에
from A to B: A에서 B까지
between A and B: A와 B 사이에

9. in front of: ~ 앞에

10. ①②③⑤ under, ④ at

11. ② next → next to

12. ⑤ he → him

13.
> 장난감 자동차는 상자 위에 있다. 그 상자는 책장 앞에 있다. 그 책장은 의자와 크리스마스트리 사이에 있다. 큰 창문 하나가 크리스마스트리 뒤에 있다.

⑤ 크리스마스트리는 책장 옆에 있으며, 책장이 의자와 크리스마스트리 사이에 있다.

14. in front of: ~ 앞에

15. behind: ~ 뒤에

UNIT 06 전치사 2 (시간, 기타)

A 1. 나는 2008년에 태어났어요.
수업은 9시에 시작해요.
겨울 방학은 12월 21일에 시작해요.
2. 당신은 8시 정각 전에 집에 와야 해요.
우리는 종종 방과 후에 야구를 해요.
그들은 파리에 일주일 동안 머물렀어요.

B 그 TV 프로그램은 동물들에 관한 것이에요.
나는 버스를 타고 학교에 가요.
나는 당신을 위해 특별한 케이크를 만들었어요.

우리는 어제 동물원에 갔어요.
나는 조부모님과 함께 살아요.

🫘 My Grammar Notes   p.79

1. in, at, on   **2.** by, for, to, with   **3.** on, on
4. to, to

Step1 Warm-Up   p.80-81

A 1. in 2. on 3. at 4. in 5. on 6. in
7. in 8. at 9. in 10. at 11. on 12. at
13. on 14. on

B 1. after 2. before 3. after 4. before
5. after

C 1. with 2. about 3. to 4. with 5. from
6. for

D 1. ⓑ 2. ⓓ 3. ⓐ 4. ⓕ 5. ⓒ 6. ⓔ

Step2 Practice   p.82-85

A 1. at 10:30 2. in 1756 3. on Tuesdays
4. in the morning 5. on his birthday
6. at night 7. On June 14

B 1. in 2. after 3. at 4. before 5. for
6. after

C 1. in 2. at 3. on 4. by 5. about
6. with 7. for 8. from 9. to
10. between

D 1. with 2. about 3. to 4. by 5. with
6. for 7. at 8. before 9. for 10. after

E 1. on 2. in 3. on 4. to 5. by 6. at

F 1. I like to go fishing with my dad.
2. Paul talked about his hobby.
3. I practice the drums from 5 to 6 p.m.
4. Andy sent a text message to his
classmates.

Step3 Grammar into Writing   p.86-87

A 1. ⓓ, I will have a party on my birthday.
  2. ⓒ, Jake went to Paris by airplane.
  3. ⓑ, Adam sent an e-mail to his friend.
  4. ⓐ, Jessica eats bread with warm milk.

B 1. 1) in, for 2) He stayed in Japan for three weeks.
  2. 1) at, in
    2) I watch TV at 8 in the evening.
  3. 1) for, after
    2) I bought this book for Tom after school.
  4. 1) with
    2) Kate wrote a letter with a new pen.

C between, at, on, in, with, for

Wrap-Up Test   p.88-90

1. ④ **2.** ② **3.** ③ **4.** ③ **5.** ③ **6.** ①
7. ④ **8.** ② **9.** ⑤ **10.** ④ **11.** about
12. with, after **13.** on **14.** I often have a cup of coffee at night.
15. Can you eat these noodles with chopsticks?

1. ④ 요일 앞에는 전치사 on을 쓴다.
2. 구체적인 시간이나 장소의 한 지점을 가리킬 때는 전치사 at을 쓴다.
3. '~ 위에'라는 장소의 의미를 나타내거나 특정한 날을 가리키는 전치사는 on이다.
4. 첫 번째 빈칸에는 파리로 간다고 했으므로 목적지를 나타내는 전치사 to를 쓰고, 비행기는 교통수단이므로 두 번째 빈칸에는 by를 쓰고, 세 번째 빈칸 뒤에는 월요일이 이어지므로 전치사 on을 쓴다.
5. 쇼 시작 10분 전에 휴대전화 전원을 껐으므로, 빈칸에는 전치사 before가 적절하다.
6. in + 오전, by + 교통수단
7. ①②③⑤ ~을 위해, ④ ~ 동안
8. ①③④⑤는 '~에, ~로'라는 의미로 가야 할 목적지를 나타내는 반면, ②는 '~에게'라는 뜻으로 행위의 대상을 가리킬 때 쓰인다.
9. about: ~에 대한
10. ① in + 계절 ② by + 교통수단 ③ in + 월 ⑤ on + 날짜
11. about: ~에 대한
12. with: ~와 함께, after: ~후에
13. on + 특정한 날
14. at + 특정 시점
15. with: ~을 가지고

UNIT 07 접속사

A 그는 젊고 부유해요.
  나는 감기에 걸려서 병원에 갔어요.

B 나는 샌드위치에 달걀과 치즈, 그리고 햄을 넣어요.
  그 영화는 길었지만 흥미로웠어요.
  당신은 어젯밤에 밖에 나갔나요, 아니면 집에 머물렀나요?
  너무 더워서, 나는 창문을 열었어요.

C 나는 아팠을 때, 일찍 잠자리에 들었어요.
  내가 오늘 아침에 일어났을 때, 오전 10시였어요.
  엄마가 집에 오시기 전에, 나는 숙제를 끝내야 해요.
  영화가 시작하기 전에, 우리는 10분의 시간이 있어요.
  숙제를 하고 난 후에 나는 밖에 나갈 거예요.
  당신이 그 책을 읽고 난 후에 제가 그걸 빌려도 될까요?

비가 많이 왔기 때문에, 그는 세차하지 않았어요.
나는 휴대폰을 잃어버려서 당신에게 전화하지
않았어요.

🫘 My Grammar Notes　　　p.93

1. 접속사　2. but, or, so, 명사, 형용사

3. when, before, because

Step1 Warm-Up　　　p.94-95

A 1. big (and) white

2. Tuesday (or) Wednesday

3. She was sad, (but) she didn't cry.

4. Let's go out (after) the rain stops.

5. I make a plan (before) I try something.

6. to travel to Europe (when) I am 20

7. It's cold outside, (so) I am going to
wear a coat.

8. I like Sunday (because) I don't have to
go to school.

B 1. and　2. but　3. or　4. but　5. so
6. and　7. so　8. or

C 1. before　2. because　3. when
4. Because　5. After　6. after　7. when
8. before

D 1. ⓓ　2. ⓐ　3. ⓑ　4. ⓕ　5. ⓔ　6. ⓒ　7. ⓖ

Step2 Practice　　　p.96-99

A 1. apples ✓ strawberries
2. diligent ✓ she　3. light ✓　4. you ✓ I'm
5. Seoul ✓ in　6. dark ✓ we　7. bad ✓ they

B 1. ①　2. ①　3. ③　4. ②　5. ①

C 1. or　2. but　3. so　4. because
5. when　6. and

D 1. and　2. but　3. after[After]　4. before
5. When[when]

E 1. When　2. before　3. because
4. when　5. after　6. but　7. so
8. before　9. because　10. After

F 1. ①　2. ②　3. ③　4. ③

G 1. after　2. she was late　3. so　4. sang
5. and　6. sweet

Step3 Grammar into Writing　　　p.100-101

A 1. because I was tired

2. but I am short

3. so I ate some ice cream

4. slowly and carefully

5. or in the afternoon

B 1. I always feel sick after I ride a roller
coaster.

2. When it is raining, I watch TV at
home.

3. I didn't wear a jacket because it was
warm.

4. Can I read a comic book before I do
my homework?

5. You must brush your teeth after you
eat chocolate.

6. When I was young, I sometimes had
terrible dreams.

C but, so, because, or

Wrap-Up Test

p.102-104

1. ④ **2.** ④, ⑤ **3.** ③ **4.** ④ **5.** ⑤ **6.** ②
7. ② **8.** ④ **9.** ③ **10.** ④
11. after[After] **12.** because he is sick
13. I had lunch before I came here.
14. I decided to speak and write in
English every day. **15.** (1) because it
is broken (2) so I can't bake cookies

1. ④ after: ~한 후에

2. ④⑤ when(~할 때)과 so(그래서)는 문장과 문장을 연결해 주는 접속사이다.

3. so(그래서)는 뒤에 사건의 결과가, because(~이기 때문에)는 뒤에 사건의 원인 혹은 이유가 서술된다.

4. but: 그러나, so: 그래서

5. 접속사 and에 연결되는 부분이 running이므로 jumping이 알맞다. 접속사 or로 연결되는 부분이 to look in the mirror이므로, go가 적절하다. 이때 앞에 to부정사의 to가 생략되었다. 접속사 but으로 연결되는 부분이 앞 문장 전체이고 의미상 반전의 내용이 적절하므로, 마지막 빈칸에는 it wasn't there가 와야 한다.

6. before는 전치사와 접속사 두 가지로 쓰일 수 있으므로, 뒤에는 (대)명사나 '주어+동사'가 올 수 있다. ②에는 주어가 없다.

7. when: ~할 때

8. ④ 접속사 or에 의해 연결되는 부분이 동사 go이므로 watching이 아닌 watch가 적절하다.

9. 의미상, '다리를 다쳤지만 병원에 가지 않았다'가 자연스러우므로 첫 번째 접속사는 but으로, '한국에 오기 전에 스페인에 있었다'가 자연스러우므로 두 번째 접속사는 Before로 고쳐야 한다.

10. ①②③⑤ ~할 때 (접속사), ④ 언제 (의문사)

11. after가 전치사로 쓰일 때는 뒤에 명사가 오고, 접속사로 쓰일 때는 뒤에 '주어+동사'가 온다.

12. because: ~ 때문에

13. before: ~하기 전에

14. 의미상 접속사 and로 연결되는 부분이 speak이므로, writing을 write로 고쳐 써야 한다. write 앞에 to부정사의 to가 생략되었다.

15. (1) 의미상, '병이 깨졌으니 이 병을 만지지 마라'가 자연스러우므로 접속사 because와 it is broken을 이용해 문장을 완성한다.

(2) 의미상, '밀가루가 없어서, 쿠키를 구울 수 없다'가 자연스러우므로 접속사 so와 I can't bake cookies를 이용해 문장을 완성한다.

UNIT 08 명령문과 제안문

🫘 My Grammar Notes

p.107

1. 동사원형 **2.** Don't **3.** ~하자, not
4. Why, How

Step1 Warm-Up

p.108-109

A 1. ⓔ 2. ⓐ 3. ⓓ 4. ⓒ 5. ⓑ

B 1. Look 2. Bring 3. Turn 4. Don't eat
5. Never go 6. Don't play
7. Never cross 8. Tell

C 1. see 2. make 3. play 4. be
5. not go 6. Let's not

D 1. Let's 2. Shall we 3. Why don't you
4. How about 5. What about
6. Let's not

Step2 Practice

p.110-113

A 1. Clean 2. Don't[Never] eat
3. Don't[Never] worry 4. Be

5. Don't[Never] sing

B 1. Let's 2. Let's 3. Let's not 4. Let's
   5. Let's 6. Let's not 7. Let's not
   8. Let's not

C 1. Why don't, go 2. Let's play
   3. Shall we 4. Let's go 5. about taking

D 1. Listen to me carefully.
   2. Let's go to the movies tonight.
   3. Don't[Never] be late for a meeting
      again.
   4. Why don't you help that little child?
   5. Wear a seat belt when you drive.

E 1. Turn 2. we take 3. Never be
   4. Don't[Never] send 5. Let's not ride
   6. Let's buy 7. What[How] about having
   8. Why don't we swim
   9. Why don't we try

F 1. Be 2. go 3. Don't be 4. Turn off
   5. Let's not 6. Don't[Never] 7. take
   8. sing 9. playing 10. What about
   11. not send 12. take 13. climb
   14. buy 15. Never drink 16. be
   17. going 18. Watch

Step3 Grammar into Writing p.114-115

A 1. Be quiet in the library.
   2. Don't eat anything late at night.
   3. Let's go skating right now.
   4. Let's not see that horror movie.
   5. Why don't you try this toast?
   6. How about traveling to Brazil?

B 1. Put the backpack on the table.
   2. What about going to Disneyland?
   3. Let's not pick these flowers.

   4. Shall we have some tea?
   5. Don't[Never] worry about that
      problem.
   6. Why don't we study together?
   7. Let's eat cookies for dessert.

C

> **Classroom Rules**
> · Keep the classroom clean.
> · Not run in the hallway.
> · Listens carefully to your teacher.
> · Let's don't fight with classmates.
> · Wash your hands before lunch.
> · Don't never use cell phones in
>   class.

   1. Never run in the hallway.
   2. Listen carefully to your teacher.
   3. Let's not fight with classmates. /
      Don't fight with classmates.
   4. Don't[Never] use cell phones in class.

Wrap-Up Test p.116-118

1. ② **2.** ③ **3.** ③ **4.** ② **5.** ⑤ **6.** ①
7. ② **8.** ④ **9.** ④ **10.** ③ **11.** ②
12. Why don't we
13. Don't play computer games late.
14. Never[Don't] move immediately
when the traffic light turns red.
15. How about stopping by my place?

1. Let's로 시작하는 제안문의 부정은 Let's 바로 뒤에 not을 붙인다.

2. 문맥상 '~하지 마라'라는 의미가 되어야 하므로 빈칸에는 Don't 또는 Never가 적절하다.

3. What about+(동)명사 ~?
   = How about+(동)명사 ~?

4. 명령문의 부정형: Don't[Never]+동사원형 ~
제안문: What[How] about+(동)명사 ~?

5. ⑤ How about 뒤에는 (동)명사가 올 수 있다.

6. Why don't you 뒤에는 동사원형이 오고, 명령문은 동사원형으로 시작한다.

7. 이가 아파 아무것도 먹을 수가 없으므로 치과의사에게 가보라는 말이 적절하다.

8. 명령문은 동사원형으로 시작한다.

9. ①②③⑤ 점심으로 피자를 주문하자. (제안문)
④ 우리 왜 점심으로 피자를 주문하지 않았니? (의문문)

10. ③ Let's eat not → Let's not eat

11. ② 수영을 하러 가자는 제안에 동의한 후에 수영을 하지 말라는 것은 어색하다.

12. Let's go ~는 Why don't we ~?로 바꿔 쓸 수 있다.

13. 명령문의 부정형: Don't[Never]+동사원형 ~

14. 명령문의 부정형: Don't[Never]+동사원형 ~

15. How about+(동)명사 ~?: ~하는 게 어때?

UNIT 09 감탄문과 부가의문문

A 그는 매우 친절해요.
→ (그는) 정말 친절하군요!
그 경기는 흥미진진해요.
→ (그 경기는) 정말 흥미진진하군요!
그녀는 매우 예쁜 소녀예요.
→ (그녀는) 정말 예쁜 소녀군요!
그 책은 재미있어요.
→ (그것은) 정말 재미있는 책이군요!

B 1. 당신은 지루해요, 그렇지 않아요?
당신은 그를 모르죠, 그렇죠?
Tom은 피자를 먹었어요, 그렇지 않아요?

그들은 피곤해요, 그렇지 않아요?
Jenny는 수영을 못해요, 그렇죠?
Jake와 나는 여기서 만날 거예요, 그렇지 않나요?

2. 그들은 지금 슬프지 않아요, 그렇죠?
Jeff는 피아노를 잘 쳐요, 그렇지 않아요?
당신은 운전할 수 있어요, 그렇지 않아요?

🫘 My Grammar Notes   p.121

1. how, what (1) How (2) 형용사, 명사
2. 부가의문문 (1) 긍정 (2) 시제 (3) 대명사

Step1 Warm-Up   p.122-123

A 1. ? 2. ! 3. ! 4. ? 5. ! 6. ? 7. ! 8. ?
9. !

B 1. What 2. How 3. What 4. What
5. How 6. How 7. What

C 1. ⓒ 2. ⓑ 3. ⓐ 4. ⓔ 5. ⓖ 6. ⓓ 7. ⓗ
8. ⓕ

D 1. isn't she 2. was he 3. doesn't he
4. didn't we 5. will you 6. can't she
7. did they 8. are they

Step2 Practice   p.124-127

A 1. ② 2. ① 3. ② 4. ② 5. ② 6. ① 7. ②

B 1. What a lazy girl!
2. What an exciting movie!
3. What a great chance it is!
4. How expensive the bag is!
5. How generous the man is!
6. How comfortable these shoes are!

C 1. ① 2. ① 3. ③ 4. ② 5. ② 6. ③

D 1. isn't it 2. does she 3. didn't he
4. can you 5. won't they 6. aren't you

E 1. can play, can't you

2. is, isn't he   3. likes, doesn't she

4. didn't get, did they

F 1. How tall   2. What a strange

3. How clear   4. What a lovely girl

5. How old

G 1. What a pretty   2. did, didn't

3. How kind   4. help, won't you

5. What a sad   6. is, isn't it

H 1. fast she   2. How stupid   3. am I

4. What a lazy   5. won't you

6. didn't they   7. can you

Step3 **Grammar into Writing**   p.128-129

A 1. How perfect   2. What delicious

3. How wide   4. can't swim, can you

5. likes, doesn't he

6. can save, can't he

B 1. 1) are, aren't you

2) You are Japanese, aren't you?

2. 1) What a brave

2) What a small puppy!

3. 1) know, does she

2) Danny doesn't know my name, does he?

4. 1) will teach, won't you

2) Mr. Choi will teach you science, won't he?

C 1. is wonderful, isn't it?

2. How beautiful the colors were! / What the beautiful colors they were!

3. What a cute squirrel! / How cute a squirrel was!

4. was an interesting experience, wasn't it?

1. ③ **2.** ⑤ **3.** ④ **4.** ④ **5.** didn't she

6. ① **7.** ① **8.** ④ **9.** ② **10.** ③ **11.** ④

12. ③ **13.** pretty the dress is

14. What a nice picture it is!

15. You can keep your promise, can't you?

1. 조동사의 긍정형 부가의문문: 조동사+대명사? 일반동사 과거형의 부정형 부가의문문: didn't+대명사?

2. 감탄을 나타내는 부분에 명사가 없을 때는 How를 이용해서, 감탄을 나타내는 부분에 명사가 있을 때는 What을 이용해 감탄문을 만든다. 세 번째 문장은 일반동사 현재형이 쓰인 긍정문이므로, 부가의문문은 부정의 형태로 쓴다.

3. 부가의문문에 didn't가 쓰였으므로 앞 문장에는 일반동사 과거형의 긍정문이 올 수 있다. ④는 be동사의 과거형이 쓰인 문장이다.

4. story는 셀 수 있는 단수명사이므로 형용사 (interesting) 앞에 a를 쓴다. 앞 문장이 과거시제이므로 부가의문문도 과거시제로 쓴다.

5. 일반동사의 과거형이 쓰인 긍정문이므로 부가의문문은 'didn't+대명사?'로 쓴다.

6. how 감탄문: How+형용사+주어+동사!

7. 앞이 부정문이므로, 부가의문문은 긍정의 형태로 쓴다. 이때 부가의문문의 어순은 'be동사+주어?'이다.

8. what 감탄문: What(+a/an)+형용사+명사(+주어+동사)!

9. ①③④⑤ How, ② What

10. ③ What amazing score! → What an amazing score!

11. ④ doesn't he → didn't he

12. ③ will을 이용하여 앞으로의 일을 묻는 말에 과거

시제(didn't)로 답하는 것은 어색하다.

13. how 감탄문: How+형용사+주어+동사!

14. what 감탄문: What(+a/an)+형용사+명사(+주어+동사)!

15. 약속을 지킬 수 있는 가능성에 대해 물었으므로 조동사 can을 이용한 긍정문을 쓰고, 부가의문문은 부정의 형태로 쓴다.

부정의문문과 선택의문문

A 그들은 유명한 가수들이지 않나요?

– 맞아요. 그들은 한국에서 매우 유명해요.

그가 이 만화책을 쓰지 않았나요?

– 아니요, 그는 그것을 쓰지 않았어요.

당신은 하늘의 별들이 보이지 않나요?

– 네, 보여요. 하늘에 별들이 많네요.

B 당신은 커피나 차를 원하나요?

– 저는 차를 원해요.

그들은 형제인가요, 친구인가요?

– 그들은 친구예요.

당신은 검정색과 흰색 중 어떤 색상을 더 좋아하나요?

– 저는 흰색을 더 좋아해요.

당신과 당신의 언니 중 누가 더 키가 큰가요?

– 제 언니가 키가 더 커요.

🌭 My Grammar Notes
p.135

1. Isn't she, Don't you, Can't you

2. or (1) or (2) Which, or, Who, or

Step1 **Warm-Up**
p.136-137

A 1. Doesn't 2. Isn't 3. Aren't 4. Don't

5. Isn't 6. Don't 7. Aren't 8. Didn't

B 1. Yes 2. they are 3. Yes 4. I can't

5. he didn't 6. she does 7. No 8. Yes

C 1. Do 2. Which 3. or 4. Who 5. or

6. Which

D 1. © 2. ⨍ 3. ⓓ 4. ⓑ 5. ⓐ 6. ⓔ

Step2 **Practice**
p.138-141

A 1. Aren't they 2. Doesn't he 3. Isn't it

4. Can't I 5. Wasn't 6. Didn't Chris

B 1. ⓑ 2. ⓐ 3. ⓓ 4. © 5. ⨍ 6. ⓔ

C 1. Aren't you 2. Don't you

3. Isn't 4. Which, or 5. Does, or

6. Who is, or 7. Is, or

8. Wasn't, Yes, was

9. Can't you, No, can't

10. Didn't you, I

D 1. you, Yes, did 2. No, it isn't

3. Yes, it is 4. No, she can't

5. Did, or 6. Which do, or

7. Does, or 8. No, he doesn't

9. Which, or 10. Which is, or

E 1. ① 2. ② 3. ② 4. ③

F 1. Isn't 2. Which 3. or 4. Doesn't

5. or 6. or 7. do

Step3 **Grammar into Writing**
p.142-143

A 1. Don't you like seafood?

2. Didn't she tell the truth?

3. Do you go to school by bus or by subway?

4. Who is your girlfriend, Emma or Olivia?

5. Which season do you like better, summer or winter?

B **1.** 1) Can't 2) Can't he eat carrots?
  2. 1) Aren't
   2) Isn't she interested in you?
  3. 1) Which, or
   2) Which do you want, cheese or butter?
  4. 1) Who, or
   2) Who planted the tree, you or Jessica?

C **1.** Which do you like better?
  2. Isn't it exciting?
  3. Don't you want some water?
  4. Yes, I do.

Wrap-Up Test

p.144-146

1. ② **2.** ④ **3.** ③ **4.** ① **5.** ② **6.** ④
7. ⑤ **8.** ② **9.** ③ **10.** ③ **11.** ④
12. Don't you like, Yes, I do
13. Which do you want, a hamburger or a sandwich?
14. Who waited for you, Jason or Lily?
15. No, I can't.

1-2. 부정의문문은 동사의 부정형을 이용하며 이때 축약형을 쓴다.

3. B의 대답으로 보아 빈칸에는 Do 또는 Don't가 들어가야 한다.

4. 빈칸 뒤 이어지는 말에 B가 A에 동의하고 있으므로 긍정의 Yes를 써서 대답한다.

5. 어떤 것이 더 좋은지 묻는 선택의문문이므로 의문사 Which가 들어가야 한다.

6. 일반동사가 쓰인 과거시제의 부정의문문이므로 첫 번째 빈칸에는 Didn't가 적절하고, 두 번째 문장은

선택의문문이므로 or가 들어가야 한다.

7. 부정의문문의 대답으로 긍정의 의미를 나타낼 때는 Yes를, 부정의 의미를 나타낼 때는 No를 쓴다.

8. 일반동사가 쓰인 과거시제의 부정의문문이므로 Didn't로 시작해야 한다.

9. ③ '당신들은 친구인가요, 자매인가요?'라는 뜻으로, be동사로 시작하는 선택의문문이 되어야 하므로 Which가 들어갈 수 없다.

10. ③ 주어가 2인칭인 일반동사의 부정의문문은 시제에 따라 Don't 혹은 Didn't로 시작한다.

11. ④ 선택의문문에는 Yes나 No로 대답할 수 없다.

12. 일반동사가 쓰인 현재시제의 부정의문문이므로 Don't로 시작한다. 이어지는 말로 보아 긍정의 대답이 와야 하므로 'Yes, I do'를 쓴다.

13. 의문사가 있는 선택의문문은 '의문사＋동사＋주어 ~, A or B?'의 어순으로 쓴다.

14. 의문사가 있는 선택의문문으로 의문사가 주어 역할을 할 때는 '의문사＋동사 ~, A or B?'의 어순으로 쓴다.

15. 주말에는 바쁘다고 했으므로 정황상 부정의 대답이 와야 한다.

CONTENTS

A ( ) 안에서 알맞은 것을 고르세요.

1 She's (strong / stronger) than me.

2 He's the (tall / tallest) boy in his school.

3 I need a (big / biggest) bag.

4 This song is (good / better) than that one.

5 This dog is very (smart / smarter).

6 This is the (longer / longest) day of the year.

B 우리말과 같은 뜻이 되도록 주어진 말을 바르게 배열하세요.

1 이 색깔은 저 색깔보다 더 어둡다.

(darker / this color / that color / is / than)

➔ _____

2 이 스프가 저 스프보다 더 맛있다.

(this soup / that soup / than / delicious / is / more)

➔ _____

3 이 나무는 정원에서 키가 가장 큰 나무이다.

(is / the / this tree / in the garden / tallest / tree)

➔ _____

4 그는 세계에서 가장 빠른 사람이다.

(is / the / he / man / fastest / in the world)

➔ _____

Words   **dark** 어두운   **delicious** 맛있는

4 Grammar Bean 4

C 우리말과 같은 뜻이 되도록 보기의 단어를 이용하여 문장을 완성하세요.

> [보기] thick   easy   many   sad   heavy   bad

1 이것이 그 책에서 가장 슬픈 이야기이다.

→ This is _____ story in the book.

2 이쪽 벽이 저쪽 벽보다 더 두껍다.

→ This wall is _____ that wall.

3 파란 테이블이 노란 테이블보다 더 무겁다.

→ The blue table is _____ the yellow table.

4 그의 건강이 전보다 나빠졌다.

→ His health is _____ before.

5 이 문제가 저 문제보다 쉽다.

→ This question is _____ that question.

6 이 가게가 저 가게보다 품목이 더 많다.

→ This store has _____ items _____ that store.

D 밑줄 친 부분을 바르게 고쳐 쓰세요.

1 Seoul is <u>bigger</u> Busan.   → _____

2 He is the <u>more</u> famous singer in Korea.   → _____

3 She is the <u>better</u> swimmer in China.   → _____

4 This computer works <u>fast than</u> that computer. → _____

5 This team has <u>many</u> players than that team.   → _____

6 This water is <u>hottest</u> than that water.   → _____

 Words   **thick** 두꺼운   **wall** 벽   **heavy** 무거운   **item** 항목   **work** 작동하다   **player** 선수

비교급과 최상급을 이용한 표현

A 우리말과 같은 뜻이 되도록 보기의 단어를 이용하여 문장을 완성하세요.

[보기] smart   much   rich   fast   more   big

1 컴퓨터는 점점 더 빨라지고 있다.

→ Computers are getting _____ and _____.

2 이 책은 저 책보다 훨씬 흥미진진하다.

→ This book is _____ more exciting than that book.

3 책을 더 많이 읽을수록 더 똑똑해진다.

→ The more books you read, the _____ you become.

4 그는 세계에서 가장 부유한 사람 중 하나이다.

→ He is one of the _____ men in the world.

5 이 게임은 점점 더 인기를 얻고 있다.

→ This game is becoming _____ and _____ popular.

6 TV는 점점 더 커지고 있다.

→ TVs are becoming _____ and _____.

B ( ) 안에서 알맞은 것을 고르세요.

1 He is (very / much) younger than her.

2 The cat was (very / more) young and weak.

3 This is one of the most interesting (show / shows) in the world.

4 She is the (more / most) beautiful actress right now.

Words   **famous** 유명한   **cell phone** 휴대전화   **actress** 여배우   **weak** 약한

C 우리말과 같은 뜻이 되도록 주어진 단어를 이용하여 문장을 완성하세요.

1 더 빨리 도착할수록 더 많은 것을 얻을 수 있다. (soon, many)

→ _____ you arrive, _____ you can get.

2 그 호수는 점점 더 커지고 있다. (large)

→ The lake is getting _____.

3 이것은 한국에서 가장 높은 건물 중 하나이다. (tall)

→ This is _____ buildings in Korea.

4 이 그림이 저것보다 훨씬 더 아름답다. (beautiful)

→ This painting is _____ than that one.

5 그 회사는 점점 더 많은 돈을 벌어들이고 있다. (money)

→ The company is earning _____.

6 이것은 올해 올림픽 대회에서 가장 흥미진진한 경기 중 하나였다. (exciting)

→ This was _____ matches in this year's Olympic Games.

D 밑줄 친 부분을 바르게 고쳐 쓰세요.

1 This cake is <u>delicious</u> than that cake. → _____

2 <u>Longer</u> shirts I wear, the shorter I look. → _____

3 His voice was becoming <u>loud and loud</u>. → _____

4 <u>Deepest</u> the sea is, the darker it becomes. → _____

5 She is <u>very</u> smarter than her sister. → _____

6 This is one of the most expensive <u>computer</u> → _____
in this store.

Words **soon** 곧 **earn** 벌다 **match** 경기 **Olympic Games** 올림픽 대회 **deep** 깊은

Grammar Test

[1-4] 주어진 단어를 이용하여 보기와 같이 문장을 완성하세요.

> [보기] (tall)
>
> I'm <u>taller</u> than my brother.
>
> I'm the <u>tallest</u> in my family.

1 (thick)

This book is _____ than that book.

This book is the _____ book in the bookstore.

2 (high)

Lucy got _____ scores than her sister.

Lucy got the _____ scores in her class.

3 (fast)

This computer is _____ than the old one.

This is one of the _____ computers in the world.

4 (good)

He understands English much _____ than you.

He understands English the _____ among the students.

[5-7] 밑줄 친 부분을 바르게 고쳐 쓰세요.

5 It is one of the most famous <u>movie</u> of all time. → _____

6 The more I eat, <u>hungrier</u> I become. → _____

7 You're <u>very</u> more beautiful than her. → _____

 Words   **bookstore** 서점   **score** 점수, 성적   **understand** 이해하다

[8-12] ( ) 안에서 알맞은 것을 고르세요.

8 I know him (better / best) than you do.

9 The story became (longer and longer / longest and longest).

10 New York is one of the (more / most) famous cities in the world.

11 She got enough rest. She feels (more / most) relaxed than before.

12 The (harder / hardest) they worked, the (more / most) money they earned.

[13-17] 우리말과 같은 뜻이 되도록 주어진 단어를 이용하여 문장을 완성하세요.

13 이번 시험은 지난 시험보다 훨씬 쉬웠다. (easy)

➜ This exam was _____ our last exam.

14 점점 더 추워지고 있다. (cold)

➜ It's getting _____.

15 내 컴퓨터는 동생의 것보다 훨씬 더 빠르다. (fast)

➜ My computer is _____ my brother's.

16 David는 점점 더 무거워졌다. (heavy)

➜ David got _____.

17 한강은 세계에서 가장 아름다운 강 중 하나이다. (beautiful)

➜ The Han River is _____ rivers in the world.

Words   enough 충분한   rest 휴식   relaxed 긴장을 푼, 느긋한

우리말과 같은 뜻이 되도록 주어진 말을 이용하여 문장을 만드세요.

18 네가 일찍 올수록, 너는 더 많은 시간을 가질 것이다. (early, come)

→ _____, the more time you'll have.

19 이것은 세계에서 가장 성공적인 소설 중 하나이다. (successful, novel)

→ _____ in the world.

20 이 가방은 저 가방보다 더 크다. (bag, big)

→ _____

21 그는 자신의 아버지보다 훨씬 키가 크다. (tall, his father)

→ _____

22 그녀는 점점 더 나은 케이크를 만들었다. (make, good cakes)

→ _____

23 네가 운동을 많이 할수록, 너는 땀을 더 많이 흘리게 된다. (exercise)

→ _____, the more you sweat.

[24-25] 빈칸에 들어갈 수 <u>없는</u> 것을 고르세요.

24

> These cookies are _____ than the candy.

① sweeter ② less healthy

③ very delicious ④ more expensive

25

> This is one of _____ buildings in Seoul.

① the tallest ② the famousest

③ the greatest ④ the most crowded

Words **successful** 성공적인 **novel** 소설 **sweat** 땀을 흘리다 **crowded** 붐비는

26 보기의 내용과 일치하는 것을 고르세요.

> [보기] Jack is stronger than John.
>   John is stronger than me.

① I'm stronger than Jack.

② John is stronger than Jack.

③ I'm the weakest among the three of us.

④ John is the strongest among the three of us.

27 올바른 문장을 고르세요.

① She has more prettier dress than me.

② I'm the smartest students in my school.

③ The more I study, better I know.

④ He became taller and taller.

28 짝지어진 문장의 의미가 서로 <u>다른</u> 것을 고르세요.

① Jenny's skirt is cheaper than my skirt.

 – My skirt is more expensive than Jenny's skirt.

② The blue jacket is smaller than the red jacket.

 – The red jacket is bigger than the blue jacket.

③ It's hotter today than yesterday.

 – It was hotter yesterday than today.

④ Danny is younger than Lily.

 – Lily is older than Danny.

Words   jacket 재킷, 상의

UNIT 03 to부정사

A 우리말과 같은 뜻이 되도록 보기의 단어를 이용하여 문장을 완성하세요.

[보기] write   do   drink   make   meet

1 나는 오늘 할 일이 많다.

→ I have many things _____ today.

2 나는 친구들을 만나기 위해 집에서 일찍 나왔다.

→ I left home early _____ my friends.

3 나는 커피 한 잔을 마시기를 원한다.

→ I want _____ a cup of coffee.

4 나는 이메일을 한 통 쓰기로 결심했다.

→ I decided _____ an e-mail.

5 나는 카레를 만들기 위해 야채를 좀 샀다.

→ I bought some vegetables _____ curry.

B ( ) 안에서 알맞은 것을 고르세요.

1 I hope (find / to find) my key.

2 I need something (eat / to eat).

3 She wants (an umbrella / to an umbrella).

4 I'm saving my money (buy / to buy) a bicycle.

5 I don't have a book (read / to read).

 leave 떠나다   **decide** 결심하다   **vegetable** 야채   **save** 저축하다

C 밑줄 친 to부정사의 의미로 알맞은 것을 보기에서 골라 그 기호를 쓰세요.

[보기] ⓐ ~하는 것, ~하기   ⓑ ~하는, ~할   ⓒ ~하기 위해, ~하려고

1   I have many problems to solve. _____

2   I want something to drink. _____

3   I raised my right hand to catch a taxi. _____

4   My job is to take beautiful photos. _____

5   I plan to visit my grandmother this vacation. _____

D 우리말과 같은 뜻이 되도록 주어진 말을 이용하여 문장을 완성하세요.

1   나는 학교에 가기 위해 버스를 탔다. (go to school)
   ➜ I took a bus _____.

2   Julia는 프랑스에 가기로 결심했다. (go to France)
   ➜ Julia decided _____.

3   나는 보내야 할 편지들을 많이 가지고 있다. (send)
   ➜ I have many letters _____.

4   나는 마실 물을 찾고 있다. (drink)
   ➜ I'm looking for water _____.

5   그는 친구에게 전화를 걸기 위해 휴대전화를 꺼냈다. (call his friend)
   ➜ He took out his cell phone _____.

6   나는 휴식을 취하고 싶다. (take a break)
   ➜ I want _____.

Words visit 방문하다   raise 들어 올리다   catch 잡다   solve 해결하다   send 보내다   look for ~을 찾다
take out 꺼내다   take a break 휴식을 취하다

A   (   ) 안에서 알맞은 것을 고르세요.

1   Brian enjoys (skiing / to ski) in the winter.

2   I finished (eating / eat) lunch.

3   We decided (taking / to take) a taxi home.

4   Suddenly she stopped (sings / singing).

5   Jake tried to avoid (answers / answering) the question.

6   My brother likes (cooks / to cook).

7   I hate (get / getting) up early in the morning.

B   보기의 단어를 이용하여 빈칸에 알맞은 동명사나 to부정사를 쓰세요.

| [보기]   hear   ask   play   buy   be |

1   I enjoy _____ cards with my friends.

2   Tommy wants _____ a movie director.

3   I hope _____ from you soon.

4   Jihoon kept _____ me questions.

5   My parents promised _____ me a dog.

Words   **suddenly** 갑자기   **avoid** 피하다   **movie director** 영화감독   **ask** 물어보다

C 우리말과 같은 뜻이 되도록 주어진 말을 바르게 배열하세요.

1 거짓말을 하는 것은 나쁘다. (bad / is / lies / telling)

→ _____

2 나는 동물원에 가는 것을 즐긴다. (enjoy / to / going / the zoo / I)

→ _____

3 나는 만화책 읽는 것을 좋아한다. (love / I / reading / comic books)

→ _____

4 그녀의 일은 학생들을 가르치는 것이다. (job / is / teaching / her / students)

→ _____

5 Julie와 함께 이야기하는 것은 재미있다. (fun / with / Julie / is / talking)

→ _____

6 Yuri는 빵 먹는 것을 좋아한다. (likes / Yuri / bread / eating)

→ _____

7 나는 안경 쓰는 것을 좋아하지 않는다. (don't / like / I / glasses / wearing)

→ _____

8 미나는 샌드위치를 만들기 시작했다.

(sandwiches / started / Mina / making)

→ _____

9 다른 나라를 방문하는 것은 신나는 일이다.

(other countries / exciting / visiting / is)

→ _____

10 패스트푸드를 먹는 것은 네 건강에 좋지 않다.

(for your health / good / eating / fast food / is / not)

→ _____

 Words　　lie 거짓말　**health** 건강　**fast food** 패스트푸드

Grammar Test

[1-8]   주어진 단어를 이용하여 빈칸에 알맞은 말을 쓰세요.

1   I want _____ to you. (talk)

2   I ran really fast _____ the bus. (catch)

3   You'll enjoy _____ the movie. (watch)

4   _____ water is good for your health. (drink)

5   He finished _____ his room. (clean)

6   She decided _____ the red coat. (buy)

7   _____ regularly is very important. (exercise)

8   I drank a cup of coffee _____ awake. (stay)

[9-13]   밑줄 친 부분이 맞으면 O, 틀리면 바르게 고쳐 쓰세요.

9   David wants <u>be</u> a doctor in the future.   →   _____

10   I like <u>go</u> skiing.   →   _____

11   Her hobby is <u>collecting</u> funny pictures.   →   _____

12   <u>Read</u> magazines is interesting.   →   _____

13   I avoided <u>to wear</u> a cap.   →   _____

Words   **regularly** 규칙적으로   **stay awake** 깨어 있다   **collect** 모으다   **magazine** 잡지

[14-18]   (   ) 안에서 알맞은 것을 고르세요.

14   We hope (to meet / meeting) you soon.

15   I like (go / going) fishing with my father.

16   She (watches / watching) TV on weekends.

17   Sending e-mails (is / are) easy.

18   I started (learn / to learn) French.

[19-24]   우리말과 같은 뜻이 되도록 주어진 단어를 이용하여 문장을 완성하세요.

19   나는 사진을 찍으러 내일 외출을 할 것이다. (take)

→   I'm going to go out tomorrow _____ pictures.

20   그는 축구를 하는 것을 즐겼다. (play)

→   He enjoyed _____ soccer.

21   나는 탄산음료를 마시는 것을 멈추었다. (drink)

→   I stopped _____ soda.

22   그녀는 너를 그녀의 사무실에서 만나길 원한다. (meet)

→   She wants _____ you in her office.

23   그는 먹을 것이 필요하다. (eat)

→   He needs something _____.

24   수학을 공부하는 것은 재미가 없다. (study)

→   _____ math isn't interesting.

Words   **soda** 탄산음료   **office** 사무실

[25-30] 우리말과 같은 뜻이 되도록 주어진 말을 이용하여 문장을 만드세요.

25 정직한 것은 중요하다. (be honest, important)

→ _____

26 그는 그 소설을 읽는 것을 끝냈다. (finish, read, the novel)

→ _____

27 그녀는 그의 편지를 기다리는 것을 포기했다. (give up, wait for)

→ _____

28 클래식 음악을 듣는 것은 도움이 된다. (listen to classical music, helpful)

→ _____

29 그는 자신의 아들을 방문하고 싶어 한다. (want, visit his son)

→ _____

30 그는 그 경기에서 이기기 위해 최선을 다했다. (do his best, win the game)

→ _____

[31-32] 빈칸에 들어갈 수 <u>없는</u> 것을 고르세요.

31

I like _____.

① books   ② reading books
③ read books   ④ to read books

32

His job is _____.

① very interesting   ② writing stories
③ to write stories   ④ writes stories

Words　honest 정직한　give up 포기하다　classical music 고전음악　helpful 도움이 되는　do one's best 최선을 다하다

33 밑줄 친 to부정사의 쓰임이 다른 하나를 고르세요.

① I hope to see you soon.

② She began to cry.

③ He got up early to go to school.

④ Do you want to go to the park?

[34-36] 올바른 문장을 고르세요.

34 ① My hobby is taking pictures of flowers.

② He gave up to send the letter.

③ Did he decide buying them?

④ Get up early is not easy.

35 ① She wanted being a lawyer.

② I enjoyed played basketball.

③ He'll finish doing his job soon.

④ I need a pen write with.

36 ① Jane loves go shopping.

② He hopes being rich.

③ He finished to write a report.

④ She began to clean the room.

 Words lawyer 변호사   report 보고서

전치사 1 (장소, 위치)

A 다음 문장에서 전치사를 찾아 O 표시하세요.

1 Water is good for our health.

2 There is no air in space.

3 Anna wrote the letter with a pen.

4 We sat on the bench.

5 My dad bought a doll for me.

6 There is a beautiful picture on the wall.

7 I will stay at home this weekend.

B 보기에서 알맞은 말을 골라 in, at, on을 이용하여 문장을 완성하세요.

[보기]	the wall	the river	the table
	the park	your coffee	the world

1 Some people are swimming _____.

2 Would you like sugar _____?

3 Let's meet _____.

4 What is the tallest building _____?

5 I want to hang the picture _____.

6 He put the newspaper _____.

 air 공기 **space** 우주 **weekend** 주말 **hang** 걸다 **put** 놓다, 두다

C 우리말과 같은 뜻이 되도록 빈칸에 알맞은 전치사를 쓰세요.

1 제가 창 옆에 앉아도 될까요?

→ Can I sit _____ the window?

2 많은 사람들이 역에서 기차를 기다리고 있다.

→ Many people are waiting for a train _____ the station.

3 그는 지금 벽 앞에 서 있다.

→ He is standing _____ the wall.

4 수영장에서는 수영복을 입어야 한다.

→ You have to wear a bathing suit _____ the pool.

5 병원 뒤에 작은 식당이 있다.

→ There's a small restaurant _____ the hospital.

D 우리말과 같은 뜻이 되도록 주어진 말을 바르게 배열하세요.

1 내 가방은 책상 아래에 있다. (is / my bag / the desk / under)

→ _____

2 꽃병에 꽃이 몇 송이 있다. (in the vase / are / there / some flowers)

→ _____

3 그 공은 침대와 벽 사이로 굴러갔다.

(the wall / the ball / between / rolled / the bed / and)

→ _____

4 Mike는 여기서 그 공원까지 운전했다.

(Mike / the park / to / drove / here / from)

→ _____

 Words   **wait for** ~를 기다리다   **bathing suit** 수영복   **pool** 수영장   **vase** 꽃병   **roll** 구르다

A ( ) 안에서 알맞은 것을 고르세요.

1 I lived in Busan (before / for) two years.

2 I take a shower (at / before) breakfast.

3 I drink a lot of water (after / at) running.

4 We played basketball (on / for) an hour.

5 We played football (after / for) school.

6 The new restaurant opens (at / on) May 2.

7 Dad gave me a present (at / on) Christmas Day.

8 Turn off your cell phone (before / from) the show.

9 The bank is open (after / from) 9 a.m. to 4 p.m.

B 빈칸에 in, at, on 중 알맞은 전치사를 쓰세요.

1 The class starts _____ 9 a.m.

2 It snowed a lot _____ January in Seoul.

3 I visit my grandmother _____ her birthday.

4 What do you usually do _____ the evening?

5 People eat turkey _____ Thanksgiving Day.

Words   **turn off** (전원을) 끄다   **show** 공연   **turkey** 칠면조 (고기)   **Thanksgiving Day** 추수감사절

C 우리말과 같은 뜻이 되도록 주어진 말을 이용하여 문장을 완성하세요.

1 우리는 월요일에 시험이 있다. (Monday)

→ We have a test _____.

2 그는 Alice를 위해 꽃 몇 송이를 샀다.

→ He bought some flowers _____.

3 우리 아빠는 아침에 신문을 읽으신다. (morning)

→ My dad reads a newspaper _____.

4 Jessica는 금발머리를 가진 소녀이다. (blond hair)

→ Jessica is a girl _____.

5 나는 자정에 잠자리에 들었다. (midnight)

→ I went to bed _____.

6 우리는 한 달 동안 그곳에 머물렀다. (a month)

→ We stayed there _____.

7 우리는 저녁 식사 후에 TV를 본다. (dinner)

→ We watch TV _____.

8 나는 12월에 태어났다. (December)

→ I was born _____.

9 Mary는 리본으로 상자를 묶었다. (a ribbon)

→ Mary tied the box _____.

10 해가 지기 전에 집으로 돌아와라. (sunset)

→ Come back home _____.

 Words **blond** 금발의 **midnight** 자정, 12시 **be born** 태어나다 **tie** 묶다 **ribbon** 리본 **sunset** 일몰

접속사

A ( ) 안에서 알맞은 것을 고르세요.

1 I liked Minsu (when / after) I was young.

2 (So / Because) I lost my wallet, I couldn't take a bus.

3 My family will go to France, Spain, (and / but) Italy on vacation.

4 Please turn off the computer (after / before) you use it.

5 Do you want pasta (or / but) pizza?

6 We have to get to the station (so / before) the train leaves.

7 Jack is short, (but / so) he can run fast.

B 보기에서 알맞은 말을 골라 빈칸에 쓰세요.

[보기]	but	so	because	when	before

1 My mother was beautiful _____ she was young.

2 You have to go home _____ it gets dark.

3 I drank a lot of water _____ I was thirsty.

4 It was very hot last night, _____ I didn't sleep well.

5 I want to play outside, _____ I have to do homework now.

C 우리말과 같은 뜻이 되도록 빈칸에 알맞은 말을 쓰세요.

1 우리 개는 작고 귀엽다.

→ My dog is small _____ cute.

2 펭귄은 새이지만, 날지 못한다.

→ Penguins are birds, _____ they are not able to fly.

3 Tom은 거짓말을 많이 해서, 그의 친구들은 그를 믿지 않는다.

→ Tom lies a lot, _____ his friends don't trust him.

4 나는 버스를 놓쳤기 때문에 학교에 지각했다.

→ I was late for school _____ I missed the bus.

5 너는 우유와 오렌지 주스 중에 무엇을 원하니?

→ Do you want milk _____ orange juice?

6 숙제를 마친 후에 너에게 전화할게.

→ I'll call you _____ I finish my homework.

7 수영을 하기 전에 준비운동을 해야 한다.

→ You have to warm up _____ you swim.

8 날씨가 너무 더워서 밖에서 놀 수가 없다.

→ It is really hot, _____ we can't play outside.

9 눈이 올 때 너는 보통 무엇을 하니?

→ What do you usually do _____ it snows?

10 그 영화를 보고 난 후에 나는 중국에 가고 싶어졌다.

→ _____ I watched the movie, I wanted to go to China.

 Words   **penguin** 펭귄   **lie** 거짓말을 하다   **trust** 믿다, 신뢰하다   **warm up** 준비운동을 하다

Grammar Test

[1-8] 보기에서 알맞은 전치사를 골라 빈칸에 쓰세요.

> [보기] between   about   on   in   with   at   after   by

1 Mr. Smith lives _____ Incheon.

2 I go to school _____ bicycle.

3 The cat was sitting _____ the tree and the black car.

4 David stayed _____ home yesterday.

5 Will you go jogging _____ me?

6 We're going to have a party _____ Christmas Day.

7 She likes to talk _____ other people's styles.

8 Let's have dinner together _____ work.

[9-13] 밑줄 친 부분을 바르게 고쳐 쓰세요.

9 His house is <u>next</u> my house. → _____

10 She turned off the TV and <u>turning on</u> the radio. → _____

11 I have to clean the room and <u>washing</u> the dishes. → _____

12 They moved from India <u>in</u> China. → _____

13 After <u>bought</u> the ticket, he watched the musical. → _____

Words   musical 뮤지컬

26 Grammar Bean 4

[14-18]   ( ) 안에서 알맞은 것을 고르세요.

14   I like vegetables, (and / but) my brother doesn't like them.

15   I have a lot of homework, (so / or) I can't go out.

16   (After / And) I had dinner, I brushed my teeth.

17   You can wait for him here (so / or) in his office.

18   I worked part-time (before / because) I needed some money.

[19-22]   우리말과 같은 뜻이 되도록 주어진 말을 바르게 배열하세요.

19   그는 오후 4시와 6시 사이에 Main 거리에 있었다.

He was (and / 4 p.m. / 6 p.m. / on Main Street / between)

➔   He was _____.

20   나는 학교 버스 앞에서 Jessie를 만났다.

I (of / in / Jessie / front / the school bus / met).

➔   I _____.

21   네가 내 말을 듣지 않을 때 나는 정말 속상하다.

I (me / you / don't / am upset / listen to / when).

➔   I _____.

22   너는 게임을 하기 전에 숙제를 해야 한다.

You (play games / do / your homework / must / you / before).

➔   You _____.

Words   vegetable 야채, 채소   work part-time 아르바이트를 하다   upset 속상한

[23-28]   우리말과 같은 뜻이 되도록 주어진 말을 이용하여 문장을 완성하세요.

23   너는 그 빨간 상자와 파란 상자 중에서 선택해야 한다.

→ You have to choose _____ the red box _____ the blue box.

24   나는 월요일에 나의 보고서를 제출했다. (Monday)

→ I handed in my report _____.

25   그는 찬물로 샤워를 한 후에 감기에 걸렸다. (take a shower)

→ _____ with cold water, he caught a cold.

26   그는 이틀 동안 누워있었다. (two days)

→ He stayed in bed _____.

27   어두워서, 나는 불을 켰다. (turn on the light)

→ It was dark, _____.

28   그녀는 화요일마다 버스를 타고 학교에 간다. (bus, Tuesdays)

→ She goes to school _____.

29   빈칸에 들어갈 수 <u>없는</u> 것을 고르세요.

> I was very tired, _____ I stayed up all night.

① after   ② when

③ but   ④ so

30   빈칸에 알맞은 것을 <u>모두</u> 고르세요. (2개)

> I put my bag _____ the table.

① on   ② for

③ next to   ④ about

Words   **hand in** 제출하다   **catch a cold** 감기에 걸리다   **stay up** 깨어 있다   **all night** 밤새도록

31 빈칸에 들어갈 말이 <u>다른</u> 하나를 고르세요.

① I want to go to the concert _____ you.

② This story is _____ my family.

③ You can listen to music _____ this watch.

④ Playing soccer _____ my friends is really fun.

[32-33] <u>틀린</u> 문장을 고르세요.

32　① She sat next to me.

② I studied German for two weeks.

③ You must finish this before meet him.

④ Thank you for helping me.

33　① I'm so happy because I passed the test.

② After lunch, I'll go to the library.

③ Tell me about your dream.

④ I usually take a trip with the East Sea.

[34-35] 빈칸에 알맞은 것을 고르세요.

34

I want to see you _____ class.

① so　　　　　　　　② before

③ when　　　　　　　④ from

35

She will go to the store and _____ some food.

① buy　　　　　　　　② buys

③ buying　　　　　　　④ bought

Words　**take a trip** 여행을 가다

A 보기에서 알맞은 말을 골라 빈칸에 쓰세요.

> [보기] turn up   go out   bring   find   meet   turn on

1 It is raining a lot. Let's not _____ today.

2 The classroom is too dark. _____ the light.

3 I'm so hungry. Please _____ me some snacks.

4 Why don't we _____ in front of the theater at 6?

5 The baby is sleeping. Don't _____ the volume.

6 This sofa is too expensive. Let's _____ another one.

B 보기의 표현을 이용하여 우리말과 같은 뜻이 되도록 영어로 쓰세요.

> [보기] move the table

1 Ryan, 탁자를 옮겨라.

→ Ryan, _____.

2 Ryan, 탁자를 옮기지 마라.

→ Ryan, _____.

3 Ryan, 탁자를 옮기자.

→ Ryan, _____.

 Words   **turn up** (볼륨 등을) 높이다   **volume** 볼륨

C 밑줄 친 부분을 바르게 고쳐 쓰세요.

1 Never <u>took</u> pictures in this museum. → _____

2 Shall we <u>going</u> hiking this weekend? → _____

3 <u>Do</u> quiet when you are in the gallery. → _____

4 Let's <u>buys</u> a present for Jimmy. → _____

5 How about <u>put</u> this lamp by the sofa? → _____

6 Why don't you <u>taking</u> a taxi? → _____

7 <u>Doesn't</u> tell him about this problem. → _____

D 우리말과 같은 뜻이 되도록 주어진 말을 이용하여 문장을 만드세요.

1 A: When will we meet?

   B: _____ (meet)
   (3시에 만나자.)

2 A: What do you want for dinner?

   B: _____ (what, order pizza)
   (피자를 주문하는 게 어때?)

3 A: Mom, can I watch TV now?

   B: _____ (finish your homework first)
   (네 숙제를 먼저 끝내렴.)

4 A: Are you okay? You look tired.

   B: _____ (worry about me)
   (내 걱정은 하지 마.)

Words **gallery** 갤러리 **lamp** 램프 **order** 주문하다 **worry** 걱정하다

감탄문과 부가의문문

A 빈칸에 알맞은 부가의문문을 쓰세요.

1 You aren't listening to me, _____?

2 Sujin likes chocolate cake, _____?

3 You are an actor, _____?

4 The girl isn't tall, _____?

5 You can solve the problem, _____?

6 You don't go to work tomorrow, _____?

7 He'll like this present, _____?

8 Sumi and Minji like their English teacher, _____?

9 Kate left last week, _____?

10 We're going to win this game, _____?

B 우리말을 영어로 바르게 옮긴 것을 고르세요.

1 그는 내 생일파티에 올 거야, 그렇지 않니?

   ① He will come to my birthday party, won't he?

   ② He won't come to my birthday party, will he?

2 곧 비가 올 거 같진 않아, 그렇지?

   ① It is going to rain soon, isn't it?

   ② It isn't going to rain soon, is it?

 solve 해결하다 **go to work** 출근하다

C 빈칸에 알맞은 말을 넣어 감탄문을 완성하세요.

1 It's a really nice day. → _____ _____ _____ day!

2 He is a very brave boy. → What a _____ _____!

3 That puppy is really small. → _____ _____ that puppy is!

4 Jenny is a really tall girl. → _____ _____ _____ girl!

5 They are very noisy. → _____ _____ they are!

D 우리말과 같은 뜻이 되도록 주어진 말을 바르게 배열하세요.

1 정말 어려운 시험이었어! (difficult / what / test / a)

→ _____

2 정말 높은 건물이군! (the building / tall / is / how)

→ _____

3 정말 재미있는 영화였어! (interesting / an / movie / what)

→ _____

4 정말 귀여운 새구나! (how / the bird / is / cute)

→ _____

5 정말 비싼 차구나! (expensive / what / an / car)

→ _____

6 정말 잘생긴 영화배우야! (movie star / handsome / what / a)

→ _____

Words **brave** 용감한 **puppy** 강아지 **noisy** 시끄러운

부정의문문과 선택의문문

A 우리말과 같은 뜻이 되도록 빈칸에 알맞은 말을 쓰세요.

1 너는 목마르지 않니?

→ _____ _____ thirsty?

2 TV를 끄지 않았니?

→ _____ _____ turn off the TV?

3 그는 너의 남자친구가 아니니?

→ _____ _____ your boyfriend?

4 너는 학교에 걸어가지 않니?

→ _____ _____ walk to school?

5 너희들은 어제 피곤하지 않았니?

→ _____ _____ tired yesterday?

B 우리말과 같은 뜻이 되도록 주어진 말을 이용하여 문장을 완성하세요.

1 그는 피아노를 못 치니? (can, play the piano)

→ _____

2 너는 이를 닦지 않았니? (brush your teeth)

→ _____

3 계란이 신선하지 않니? (the egg, fresh)

→ _____

4 너는 안경이 필요하지 않니? (need, glasses)

→ _____

  thirsty 목마른   **fresh** 신선한

C 우리말과 같은 뜻이 되도록 주어진 말을 바르게 배열하세요.

1 너희들은 학교에 버스를 타고 가니 아니면 자전거를 타고 가니?

(by bike / do / you / go to school / by bus / or)

→ _____

2 Dan과 Nate 중에 너는 누구를 더 좋아하니?

(do / you / better / who / like / Dan or Nate)

→ _____

3 디저트로 케이크와 과일 중에 너는 어떤 것을 원하니?

(want for dessert / you / do / which / or / fruit / cake)

→ _____

4 테니스와 배드민턴 중에서 너는 어떤 운동을 더 잘하니?

(tennis / badminton / or / sport / which / do / play better / you)

→ _____

D 밑줄 친 부분을 바르게 고쳐 쓰세요.

1 Which is your hobby, reading <u>and</u> skiing? → _____

2 <u>What</u> is your cousin, Jack or Jill? → _____

3 <u>Who</u> country did you go to, Korea or Japan? → _____

4 Isn't she your sister?

– <u>Yes, she is.</u> She's my friend. → _____

5 Don't you like math?

– <u>Yes, I don't.</u> I'm very good at math. → _____

6 Can't she drive a car?

– <u>No, she can't.</u> She is a good driver. → _____

Words   **dessert** 디저트   **green tea** 녹차   **cousin** 사촌   **be good at** ~을 잘하다

Grammar Test

[1-6] 다음 문장을 보기와 같이 괄호 안의 지시에 따라 바꿔 쓰세요.

> [보기] She has beautiful hair. (what 감탄문)
> → <u>What beautiful hair!</u>

1 You must not be late again. (명령문)
→ _____

2 You know my e-mail address. (부정의문문)
→ _____

3 This soup is delicious. (how 감탄문)
→ _____

4 You knew his secret. (부가의문문)
→ _____

5 Let's clean the room together. (why don't we 제안문)
→ _____

6 Are you from Australia? Are you from Canada? (선택의문문)
→ _____

[7-10] 밑줄 친 부분을 바르게 고쳐 쓰세요.

7 <u>Doesn't</u> talk with your friends during class. → _____

8 Which do you want, water <u>and</u> juice? → _____

9 Jim is your brother, <u>doesn't</u> he? → _____

10 What a <u>cute children</u>! → _____

Words **address** 주소 **during** ~ 동안

Grammar Bean 4

[11-16] 빈칸에 알맞은 말을 넣어 대화를 완성하세요.

11 A: Aren't you late for school?

B: _____, I'm not late.

12 A: _____ amazing!

B: Yes, the show was really great.

13 A: _____ a beautiful day!

 B: Yes, it really is.

14 A: How _____ going to the gallery by bus?

B: That's a good idea.

15 A: You don't understand me, _____ you?

B: Honestly, no.

16 A: _____ is better, these shoes or those shoes?

B: These look better than those.

[17-19] 우리말과 같은 뜻이 되도록 주어진 말을 바르게 배열하세요.

17 얼마나 멋진 노래인가! (a / what / song / wonderful)

➔ _____

18 그녀는 사랑스러워, 그렇지 않니? (she / she / is / isn't / lovely)

➔ _____

19 오늘 밤에 영화 보러 갈래요? (to / tonight / we / the movies / go / shall)

➔ _____

Words honestly 솔직히   **amazing** 놀라운   **wonderful** 멋진   **lovely** 사랑스러운   **go to the movies** 영화 보러 가다

[20-25] 우리말과 같은 뜻이 되도록 주어진 말을 이용하여 문장을 만드세요.

20 말하기와 쓰기 중에 어느 것이 더 쉽니? (easy, speaking, writing)

➜ _____

21 너무 많이 걱정하지 마. (worry too much)

➜ _____

22 그녀는 우리의 편지를 받지 않았니? (receive our letter)

➜ _____

23 얼마나 웃긴 영화인지! (a funny movie)

➜ _____

24 너는 그곳에 가지 않을 거지, 그렇지? (will, go there)

➜ _____

25 그 책을 사지 말자. (let's, buy the book)

➜ _____

[26-27] 문장의 의미가 <u>다른</u> 하나를 고르세요.

26 ① What a wonderful story!

② It's a very wonderful story.

③ What is a wonderful story?

④ What a wonderful story it is!

Words　　　**receive** 받다

27　① How about visiting the office?

② Why did we visit the office?

③ What about visiting the office?

④ Let's visit the office.

[28-29]　틀린 문장을 고르세요.

28　① What great performances!

② Why don't you learn Japanese?

③ Can't you be quiet for a while?

④ Let's don't go to Joe's Restaurant.

29　① Judy told the truth, didn't it?

② Which color do you like, red or black?

③ Shall we talk about the problem?

④ Why don't we have lunch together?

30　대화가 어색한 것을 고르세요.

① A: Why don't you read this book? It's great.
　 B: Oh, okay. I'll read it.

② A: Why do you see a doctor?
　 B: That's a good idea.

③ A: Don't you hear that sound?
　 B: Yes, I can hear something.

④ A: You called Joan, didn't you?
　 B: No, I didn't. I called James.

Words　**performance** 공연　**truth** 사실

UNIT 01 비교급과 최상급

A 1 stronger 2 tallest 3 big 4 better
5 smart 6 longest

B 1 This color is darker than that color.
2 This soup is more delicious than that soup.
3 This tree is the tallest tree in the garden.
4 He is the fastest man in the world.

C 1 the saddest 2 thicker than
3 heavier than 4 worse than
5 easier than 6 more, than

D 1 bigger than 2 most 3 best
4 faster than 5 more 6 hotter

UNIT 02 비교급과 최상급을 이용한 표현

A 1 faster, faster 2 much 3 smarter
4 richest 5 more, more
6 bigger, bigger

B 1 much 2 very 3 shows 4 most

C 1 The sooner, the more
2 larger and larger
3 one of the tallest
4 much more beautiful
5 more and more money
6 one of the most exciting

D 1 more delicious 2 The longer
3 louder and louder 4 The deeper
5 much 6 computers

Grammar Test ▸▸Unit 1~2

1 thicker, thickest 2 higher, highest
3 faster, fastest 4 better, best 5 movies
6 the hungrier 7 much 8 better
9 longer and longer 10 most 11 more
12 harder, more 13 much easier than
14 colder and colder 15 much faster than
16 heavier and heavier
17 one of the most beautiful
18 The earlier you come
19 This is one of the most successful novels
20 This bag is bigger than that bag.
21 He is much taller than his father.
22 She made better and better cakes.
23 The more you exercise
24 ③ 25 ② 26 ③ 27 ④ 28 ③

UNIT 03 to부정사

A 1 to do 2 to meet 3 to drink 4 to write
5 to make

B 1 to find 2 to eat 3 an umbrella 4 to buy
5 to read

C 1 ⓑ 2 ⓑ 3 ⓒ 4 ⓐ 5 ⓐ

D 1 to go to school 2 to go to France
3 to send 4 to drink
5 to call his friend 6 to take a break

UNIT 04 동명사

A 1 skiing 2 eating 3 to take 4 singing
5 answering 6 to cook 7 getting

B 1 playing 2 to be 3 to hear 4 asking
5 to buy

C 1 Telling lies is bad.
2 I enjoy going to the zoo.
3 I love reading comic books.
4 Her job is teaching students.
5 Talking with Julie is fun.
6 Yuri likes eating bread.
7 I don't like wearing glasses.
8 Mina started making sandwiches.
9 Visiting other countries is exciting.
10 Eating fast food is not good for your
health.

Grammar Test ▸▸Unit 3~4

1 to talk 2 to catch 3 watching
4 Drinking 5 cleaning 6 to buy
7 Exercising 8 to stay 9 to be
10 going[to go] 11 ○ 12 Reading
13 wearing 14 to meet 15 going 16 watches
17 is 18 to learn 19 to take
20 playing 21 drinking 22 to meet
23 to eat 24 Studying
25 Being honest is important.
26 He finished reading the novel.
27 She gave up waiting for his letter.
28 Listening to classical music is helpful.
29 He wants to visit his son.

30 He did his best to win the game.
31 ③ 32 ④ 33 ③ 34 ① 35 ③ 36 ④

UNIT 05 전치사 1 (장소, 위치)

A 1 for 2 in 3 with 4 on 5 for 6 on
7 at

B 1 in the river 2 in your coffee
3 at the park 4 in the world
5 on the wall 6 on the table

C 1 next to 2 at 3 in front of
4 in[at] 5 behind

D 1 My bag is under the desk.
2 There are some flowers in the vase.
3 The ball rolled between the bed and the
wall.
4 Mike drove from here to the park.

UNIT 06 전치사 2 (시간, 기타)

A 1 for 2 before 3 after 4 for 5 after
6 on 7 on 8 before 9 from

B 1 at 2 in 3 on 4 in 5 on

C 1 on Monday 2 for Alice 3 in the morning
4 with blond hair 5 at midnight
6 for a month 7 after dinner
8 in December 9 with a ribbon
10 before sunset

UNIT 07 접속사

A 1 when 2 Because 3 and 4 after
5 or 6 before 7 but

B 1 when 2 before 3 because 4 so 5 but

C 1 and 2 but 3 so 4 because 5 or
6 after 7 before 8 so 9 when 10 After

Grammar Test ▸▸Unit 5~7

1 in 2 by 3 between 4 at 5 with 6 on
7 about 8 after 9 next to 10 turned on
11 wash 12 to
13 he bought 또는 buying 14 but 15 so
16 After 17 or 18 because
19 on Main Street between 4 p.m. and 6 p.m.
20 met Jessie in front of the school bus
21 am upset when you don't listen to me
22 must do your homework before you play
games
23 between, and 24 on Monday
25 After he took a shower
26 for two days
27 so I turned on the light
28 by bus on Tuesdays
29 ④ 30 ①, ③ 31 ② 32 ③ 33 ④ 34 ②
35 ①

UNIT 08 명령문과 제안문

A 1 go out 2 Turn on 3 bring 4 meet
5 turn up 6 find

B 1 move the table 2 don't move the table
3 let's move the table

C 1 take 2 go 3 Be 4 buy 5 putting
6 take 7 Don't[Never]

D 1 Let's meet at 3.
2 What about ordering pizza?
3 Finish your homework first.
4 Don't worry about me.

UNIT 09 감탄문과 부가의문문

A 1 are you 2 doesn't she 3 aren't you
4 is she 5 can't you 6 do you 7 won't he
8 don't they 9 didn't she 10 aren't we

B 1 ① 2 ②

C 1 What a nice 2 brave boy 3 How small
4 What a tall 5 How noisy

D 1 What a difficult test!
2 How tall the building is!
3 What an interesting movie!
4 How cute the bird is!
5 What an expensive car!
6 What a handsome movie star!

UNIT 10 부정의문문과 선택의문문

A 1 Aren't you 2 Didn't you 3 Isn't he
4 Don't you 5 Weren't you

B 1 Can't he play the piano?
2 Didn't you brush your teeth?
3 Isn't the egg fresh?
4 Don't you need glasses?

C **1** Do you go to school by bus or by bike?

2 Who do you like better, Dan or Nate?

3 Which do you want for dessert, cake or fruit?

4 Which sport do you play better, tennis or badminton?

D **1** or　**2** Who　**3** Which　**4** No, she isn't.

5 Yes, I do.　**6** Yes, she can.

Grammar Test ▸Unit 8~10

1 Don't[Never] be late again.

2 Don't you know my e-mail address?

3 How delicious (this soup is)!

4 You knew his secret, didn't you?

5 Why don't we clean the room together?

6 Are you from Australia or Canada?

7 Don't[Never]　**8** or

9 isn't　**10** cute child　**11** No　**12** How

13 What　**14** about　**15** do　**16** Which

17 What a wonderful song!

18 She is lovely, isn't she?

19 Shall we go to the movies tonight?

20 Which is easier, speaking or writing?

21 Don't worry too much.

22 Didn't she receive our letter?

23 What a funny movie!

24 You won't go there, will you?

25 Let's not buy the book.

26 ③　**27** ②　**28** ④　**29** ①　**30** ②

그래머빈 With Workbook

Beginning! 영어 초보자들을 배려한 쉽고 간결한 문법 설명
Easy! 쉽고 재미있는 다양한 연습 문제 수록
Active! 문법 학습을 통한 자신 있는 영어 쓰기
New! 예비중 새내기를 위한 중등 내신 대비용 문항 확충

10분 만에 끝내는 영어 수업 준비!

NETutor

NE Tutor는 NE능률이 만든 대한민국 대표 영어 티칭 플랫폼으로
영어 수업에 필요한 모든 콘텐츠와 서비스를 제공합니다.

www.netutor.co.kr

NE Tutor
- 튜터 Mall
- 교재 / 수업자료
- 커리큘럼
- 스마트 문제뱅크
- E-Book
- 스마트 클래스

─ ☐ ✕

• 전국 영어 학원 선생님들이 뽑은 NE Tutor 서비스 TOP 4! •

교재 수업자료 ELT부터 초중고까지 수백여 종 교재의 부가자료, E-Book,
어휘 문제 마법사 등 믿을 수 있는 영어 수업 자료 제공

커리큘럼 대상별/영역별/수준별 교재 커리큘럼 & 영어 실력에 맞는
교재를 추천하는 레벨테스트 제공

NELT **한국 교육과정 기반의 IBT 영어 테스트** 어휘+문법+듣기+독해 영역별 영어
실력을 정확히 측정하여, 전국 단위 객관적 지표 및 내신/수능 대비 약점 처방

문법 문제뱅크 NE능률이 엄선한 3만 개 문항 기반의 문법 문제 출제 서비스,
최대 50문항까지 간편하게 객관식&주관식 문제 출제

NE_Tutor